ALIENATION AND THE BODY IN A RACIST SOCIETY:

A Study of the Society that Invented Soweto

ALIENATION AND THE BODY IN RACIST SOCIETY:

A Study of the Society that Invented Soweto

by Noel C. Manganyi

NOK Publishers   New York • London • Lagos

First published in the United States of America
by NOK Publishers International Ltd.

and simultaneously
by NOK Publishers (Nigeria) Ltd.

Library of Congress Catalog Card Number 74-81854
International Standard Book Number 0-88357-053-x

Printed in the United States of America.

CONTENTS

No worst, there is none. Pitched past pitch of grief,
More pangs will, schooled at forepangs, wilder wring.
Comforter, where is your comforting?
Mary, mother of us, where is your relief?
My cries heave, herds-long; huddle in a main, a chief-woe,
World-sorrow; on an age-old anvil wince and sing-
Then lull, then leave off. Fury had shrieked "No lingering."
Let me be fell: force I must be brief!
O the mind, mind has mountains; cliffs of fall
Frightful, sheer, no-man-fathomed. Hold them cheap
May who ne'er hung there. Nor does long our small
Durance deal with that steap or deep. Here! creep,
Wretch, under a comfort serves in a whirlwind: all
Life death does end and each day dies with sleep.

G. M. Hopkins

ACKNOWLEDGEMENTS

This book was completed during the first year of my term as Fellow in the Department of Psychiatry of the Yale School of Medicine. I profited greatly from stimulating discussions with colleagues, particularly those at the Connecticut Mental Center with whom I have had a continuing relationship throughout my stay at Yale University.

Prof. Daniel Levinson, friend and esteemed colleague, deserves special thanks for having read the manuscript in its entirety. He was generous both with his time and suggestions which were helpful in refining the quality of the finished product. My stay at Yale was made possible by a grant from the Ford Foundation, supported by additional funds from the Department of Psychiatry. I reserve special thanks for the administrations of these two institutions. Special thanks also to Mrs. Elizabeth Bertier, secretary to the Chief Psychologist at the Connecticut Mental Health Center for her contribution in the preparation of the manuscript.

CHAPTER I

The Edge of the Precipice

. . . .
I did
nothing certain
they tell me
I believe it is
a murder
something radical
a murder
a physical negation
a final no . . . no indeed
there in his bath tub
I saw his cheeks heave
crying for mercy
killed a prime minister
not a non-descript
said no on the sharp edge of a dagger
a precious little dream . . . .

The above is an excerpt from a sketch entitled *Mashangu's Dream*, written in 1973. With a sense of relief I read later that Cesaire had grappled with a similar experience. In his case, the experience emerged as follows (Fanon, 1967):

We broke down the doors. The master's room was wide open. The master's room was brilliantly lighted, and the master was there, quite calm ... and we stopped.... He was the master.... I entered. "It is you," he said to me, quite calmly.... It was I. It was indeed I, I told him, the good slave, the faithful slave, the slavish slave, and suddenly his eyes were two frightened cockroaches on a rainy day.... I struck, the blood flowed: That is the only baptism I remember today (p. 198).

At first, these murders or assassinations would appear so final as to justify a sense of jubilation. "It was I. It was indeed I." The ecstacy that oozed out of this absolute negation of a white man both in myself and the "other" did not last as long as I had anticipated. One bold stroke was insufficient. It was not enough. My restlessness continued. When I took that imagined leap, I had no idea what was to follow. Only at the beginning of an important search, I was probably seduced by a spurious appearance of finality. I and the white man, the master, must both be killed. My one advantage was an earlier regeneration: "It is indeed I." He (the white man) must find his "I" and affirm its reality for both of us. Once I had commited the murder, I could talk to myself, and pursue the endless search. In a sketch entitled *A Soliloquy* I heard myself saying:

> there were no compelling reasons
> to say when-why I felt outraged by an impudent curiosity
> about me as blackness
> when there were doubts
> questions about integrity and respect for property
> about my motives when confronted in the dark
> with Vorster's[1] daughters
> there were no reasons to keep a diary
> saying when I got married and why
> when I felt like dying and why
> Moravia did that you know
> for good reasons

2

I could have kept one
when I knew how to write and say yes
a radical inconsistency since I could not say no
as I did say yes
no need for concern since the diary would
could have been about myself
an approximate
second order reality
indeed what has to be confronted
destroyed as it is recognized
at once is I
being me is problematic
me-ness
all those details
all here
in this bundle
a thirty-three year old heap
dog-vomit and pearls in a high-rise dumping ground
surprises for all and sundry
I-me
dialectical as being
obeying a principle of opposition
self-confrontation
a manner of presenting me to you
to confront me
you have to look me in the eyes
want to see me open
available for you to take in
to devour in a moment of exaltation
destroy me by moulding me to size
in the ventricles of your heart
destroy me
cut me to size for your pulsating heart
make me exist for you
confirm you in your being
destroy me to destroy yourself
recreating both me-ness and you-ness
in exaltation
if you will not
will not cut yourself open

destroy yourself
me-ness remains illusive
an idea requiring confirmation
on those singular occasions when I have
mutilated myself here and there
threatened to open up a great deal
cease being an idea
there have been disasters and scandals
at mid-night
retreating steps in a distant darkness
these wounds never heal you know
the whole body
me-ness
must be opened dissected
healed in a recreation destroying the idea
life's fugitives
dare not go beyond the idea
fugitives
leave me dangling in mid-air
between the idea and me-ness
me-ness in an engulfing embrace
quicksand that shifts with the tide
me-ness out there clutching at somebody's arms
me-ness out there moistening cracked lips
me-ness out there kindling fires on our finger tips
this bundle at thirty-three
a body that betrays me wherever I go
curiosity and scorn
that say look at him
he must be over thirty
so black
could be a car thief
a rapist
name it if you will
likely to be one of those
this black body
always out there in the fore-front
telling all and sundry what I may not be
should not be
could not be

once I tried fervently
to proclaim with gusto
to make a clean sweep
scrab this darkness which surrounds me
prayed with my eyes closed
poked at my food with forks and knives
grappled with Hegelianism
the stage had been set
I did not know
for a knock-about tragic-comedy
I
like Sisyphus
kept scrabing at a darkness that would not yield
the garbage collector applauded
the politicians threatened
liberals had a hearty laugh
I
like Sisyphus kept pushing
while ladies gloated over my shoulders
one day
Camus came to my rescue[2]

      "It happens that the stage-sets collapse.
      Rising, tram, four hours of work, meal
      sleep and Monday, Tuesday, Wednesday,
      Thursday, Friday and Saturday, according
      to the same rhythm—this path is easily
      followed most of the time. But one day
      the "why" arises and everything begins in
      that weariness tinged with amazement."

when that "why" surfaced
I made a few speeches
wrote a few paragraphs
went on a rampage
in the sizzling night spots of Europe and the New World
there had to
must be
incontestable evidence
somewhere
in the mortar of the pillars of St. Peter's cathedral
or the sinews of the majestic Pentagon

an organizing principle
a rationale
some explanation of my Sisyphian act
like in everything else
I was led to believe
in a prime mover out there in the horizon
in a fading whiteness
now I know
that prime mover for me
the fountain-head
is here in this darkness
I will not stay in mid-air
between the idea and me-ness
me-ness must be opened
healed in a recreation destroying the idea
if you will not cut your whiteness open
destroy yourself
me-ness will remain illusive
you-ness and me-ness
ideas requiring confirmation. . . .

What is behind this restlessness; this murderous impulse? What kind of conditions create a black man who could proclaim: "However painful it may be for me to accept this conclusion, I am obliged to state it: For the black man there is only one destiny. *And it is white.*"[3]

When one is confronted with the challenge of thriving in a racist society, statistics or "facts" are, to say the least, an innocent conceit of those who have never been on the edge of the precipice—a kind of terror captured by Hopkins in his characteristically poignant fashion.[4] To want to commit murder and rejoice does not represent a deviant sensibility within race supremacist cultures. For, whatever else one may prefer to believe, racism—particularly against blacks—is thriving in Southern Africa and elsewhere. In France, for example, race-inspired disturbances were reported recently in the French city of Marseilles (E. Sheehan, *New York Times,* December 9, 1973).

6

The existence of individuals and groups who are anti-Semite or Negrophobes requires no documentation; among them are Nobel Prize laureates, protected by a singular kind of distinction.[5] Others, more subtle, talk in terms of black neo-racism or counter-racism.[6] Mrs. Betsie Verwoed, widow of a former South African prime minister, recently exhorted white mothers in that country to inculcate separatist and racist attitudes in their children at the earliest possible age. She clinched her argument by referring to the characteristic smells of blacks (Johannesburg *Star,* November 24, 1973). There is no denying that these rumblings from various parts of the world represent the tip of the racism iceberg.

A great many people, most of them, silent, still harbor some admiration for Hitler and his methods. The time for complacency about racism is not yet within sight and may not be within sight for a considerable time to come. A world war and gas chambers were needed to convince many that anti-Semitism is a deadly evil. Contemporary society, is witnessing similar indifference towards blacks, who have no choice but to interpret this indifference as expressive of a conspiracy that continues to support totalitarian and racist regimes in Southern Africa.[7]

In order to keep the problem of racism in the mainstream of the contemporary consciousness, a specific line of inquiry is adopted here. Some levels of reality are illusive to formal psychological methods (scientific method). Dealing with such levels of reality, the artist enjoys decided advantages over the scientist. The artist's methods are less ideological since they are more attuned to the dynamic character of reality. The artist has to be responsive to the demands of reality on his methods and becomes by this very fact less subject to reductionism. These considerations have created room for stylistic and other irregularities which may become evident in the course of the present study. Where

7

these occur, they were a response to the specific demands of a particular moment in the study. So, for example, the sketches may be seen as dealing with realities that could be more effectively presented in this form than in a technical sociopsychological form characteristic of other sections of this study.

By introducing this study with references to the terrors of the great leap to *metaphysical murder,* it is possible to strike directly at the core of one of the main concerns of the study: alienation. Alienation is the virus which has to be destroyed in both the self and the other before a higher level of creative integration or situatedness in the world becomes an existential possibility. The line of inquiry is a psychophenomenological one, directed at the study of alienation and racism, viewed from the vantage point of the body-world. Put in another way, the approach here is that of a psychologist who thinks and conceptualizes psychosocial reality in a phenomenological way (van den Berg, 1953). Emphasis is placed on "radical reflection" because this is one of the tools used in the study of reality. This posture is coupled with a deliberate devotion to reality as opposed to the charismatic "scientific facts" of psychological scientism.

It should be evident that the author has been influenced by a number of important traditions ranging from experimental psychology through psychoanalysis, to what has been described as *psychohistory* or historical psychology. To these traditions must be added a philosophical orientation which may be described as existential-phenomenological. When these traditions are blended within the context of analysis of complex problems, a transposition of concepts from one tradition to another is difficult to avoid. Such difficulties arise with certain predictability in discussions of a social-psychological character based on concepts which owe their primary origins to psychoanalysis. Late in his career, Freud is known to have been

8

moving in the direction of the sociocultural, a lead which was not followed in any systematic or consistent way by either his detractors or his devotees. It will suffice to keep these difficulties in mind as we make the theoretical jumps demanded by the reality we are trying to grapple with.

In order to establish and understand the important relationships that exist between the body, alienation and racism, and because of theoretical limitations in current psychological formulations of the self-system, it is imperative to begin by establishing the fact that it is possible to talk about the body in a psychologically meaningful language. This is done not merely to establish this fact but also because more theoretical thinking is needed along these lines. The only aspects considered are those necessary for the development of a working conceptual scheme around the body-world to make the rest of this study understandable.[8]

A number of authors have presented formulations intended to relate racism to experiences and fantasies about the body: Hamilton (1964); Kubie (1965); Pinderhughes (1969); and Fisher (1973). Kovel (1970) offered a detailed, inclusive conceptual framework by integrating the psychoanalytic notions of anality and the Oedipal matrix into a psychohistorical context. Apart from Fisher, others have written within the confines of psychoanalytic thinking. Other than psychoanalysis's concern with the erogenous zones of the body, developmental psychology has been notably silent about the body and has tended, like most of advanced society, to treat the body as a holy cow—sacred yet unpalatable.[9] It is to be shown how it is indeed possible to move beyond the limitations of these vocabularies to a perspective which had its primary origins in neuropsychology and neurosurgery.

Central to the tradition about the body preferred here, is the concept of *body image,* briefly defined as the *mental representation* of one's body. This representation of one's

9

body integrates both the somatic and psychic aspects of one's self and mediates transactions between the individual and his environment.[10] Schilder (1935) understood the significance of this internal or mental representation of the body and made the point that understanding and explaining this psychological representation should be one of the priorities of psychology.

Schilder was expressing a concern firmly grounded in medical practice and reported to have originated from the work of a sixteenth century surgeon, Ambroise Pare. He described what has come to be known as the *amputation phantom*. The phantom is singularly important in any attempt to understand the idea of body image. The classical phantom sensation is a false perception, experienced by the majority of patients as a vivid presence of the whole or part of an organ after amputation. Its incidence is placed as high as 98 percent of cases of amputation (Kolb, 1959). The duration of the phantom state is variable, lasting for only short periods in some cases to several years in others. Although the phantom experience generally involves the whole affected extremity, the patient is usually more aware of and more sensitive to the distal portions of the phantom body part. Phantom sensations have been classified into three categories (Kolb, 1962). The first is described as a "mild tingling" sensation; second is a transitory but strong pin-and-needle sensation; the third is often described by patients as "twisting," "burning" or "itching."

After Pare's initial description of the amputation phantom, questions emerged relating to the possible basis or origin of phantom experiences. There appear to be two necessary and sufficient conditions for the development of a phantom state after amputation. The first condition relates to the developmental status of the body's internal representation—integration and consolidation of the body image into the self-system as personal identity. It establishes

10

age as an important factor not only with regard to the evolution of the phantom state but also in determining an individual's adjustment to its existence. Some experimental work has shown that phantoms rarely develop in children before the fourth birthday (Simmel, 1962). After the age of four, the incidence of phantom sensations increases with age and becomes predictable at eight years of age and above. A report by Jalavisto (1950) also suggests that adaptation to phantom experiences occurs more readily and more quickly in younger amputees than in older subjects.[11] A second condition concerns the suddenness of amputation of a body part. Phantom body parts rarely develop in cases of slowly developing losses.

In attempting to deal with the enigma of the amputation phantom, the idea emerged that the body had an organized internal representation. Henry Head (Schilder, 1935), a British neurologist, considered body representation, during individual development, to assume the form of a *postural schema* (model) of the body. He maintained that each individual develops a *postural schema* (an internal representation of the body) which mediates directionality in terms of up-down, left-right, back-front; posture, movement and apperception of locality beyond the physical limits of the body. This schema develops as a result of a progressive integration of standardized bodily postures which provide the individual with implicit knowledge of his body.[12]

The problem of body representation which assumed such importance for Schilder was accorded special significance in medical practice. In neurology and neurosurgery, the amputation phantom had become an intriguing problem. Interest also became deflected to other conditions believed to be related to different disturbances of body representation. Gerstmann (1940, 1942, 1957, 1958), for example, created a heated debate by insisting on the authenticity of the Gerstmann Syndrome, a questionable

11

organic syndrome which he considered for a long time to be symptomatic of a disturbance of body representation. Other disturbances such as those involving denial of illness in cases of paralysis became well documented (Critchley, 1953). A great deal of research on body representation was generated by these problems.[13]

Besides these organic conditions, an important disorder in body experience, described as *depersonalization,* has been associated with the most diverse conditions. Since its introduction by Dugas (Gladstone, 1947) towards the end of the nineteenth century, the term has come to be nonspecific in its general usage. It is now used in a number of contexts particularly with reference to certain experiences in schizophrenia, temporal lobe epilepsy and hysteria. The character of depersonalization may be illustrated by a dramatic example relating to the effects of LSD, described in a case report by Stern and Robbins (1969):

> A 21 year old woman was admitted to the hospital with her lover. He had had a number of LSD experiences and had convinced her to take it to make her less constrained sexually. About half an hour after the ingestion of approximately 200 mcg., she noticed that the bricks in the wall began to go in and out and that light affected her strangely. She became frightened when she realized that she was unable to distinguish her body from the chair she was sitting on or from her lover's body. Her fear became marked after she thought that she would not get back into herself (p. 58).

Attention has been given to these conditions not only to suggest a historical development of the notion of an internal representation of the body but also to make another point. The body which may be experienced as very intimate and personal in some situations may also be experienced as alien, incomplete, unusually heavy or simply lifeless. Put in another way, the ego has the capacity for a kind of dissocia-

12

tion or distancing. At certain times, one's body may be experienced as fully constellated into a unitary personal identity or it may be objectified and "thingified". Estrangement from one's body may arise from distress situations; in which the body is experienced as strange or lifeless as in the case of organically induced conditions. But in the culture of alienation more subtle and endemic forms of estrangement from the body exist which become even more complex and malignant in racist societies. This culturally induced estrangement from the body will be the main concern within the general contexts of alienation and racism for the rest of this inquiry.

Important implications for the theory of body representation emerge from what is currently known about phantom limb phenomena. The primary feature of these phenomena appears to be a notable "resistance" to achieving a necessary restructuring (reintegration) of the body *gestalt* into a self-system that has an essentially disrupted internal consistency. It is as though, in the face of shattering reality, the patient continues to experience a self-representation based on a previous, and now dysfunctional, integration of the body-ego. The adaptive value of this denial of change and its isolation from consciousness appears to be one of ensuring that the individual's sense of "oneness," "sameness" and "continuity" is not disrupted.[14]

Issues of body representation will be taken up more fully in later sections. The intention here has been to present a vocabulary to cover the psychological reality of the body in more than the psychoanalytic concept of erogenous zones. It has been necessary to show, without much of a digression into the extensive body image literature, that the body may be conceptualized as having an inclusive gestalt or internal representation with complex internal relations, affects and boundary features that reflect equal complexity. The body in its internal representation shares the structural-functional

13

attributes of all the other internal representations and ego-object relations.

Once the complexity of internal representations and ego-object relations is recognized it becomes clear that both idiomatic (individual) and sociocultural (interpersonal) elements converge and play a dominant role in the development of the internal representation of the body. In moving from considerations involving the purely individual body image or individual schema to the social-psychological level of an analysis of alienation and racism, it became apparent that it was necessary to posit an additional concept of body representation to reflect the radical influence of society (socialization) during individuation. This is what is later described and discussed as the *sociological schema*. By 1935, Schilder had begun to include what he described as the "sociology" of the body image in his formulations. This lead has not been followed in any serious manner, although Fisher (1973) started to make tentative moves in this direction.

The language of body representation makes it possible to talk and write about the individual and societal aspects of the body-world. The notions of the individual and sociological schemata help in dealing with the complexities of body experience in conditions of alienation. In effect, popular notions about racism and skin color make little sense because the idea of "skin color" is based on an inadequate recognition of the complexities of the individual's body-world. It makes better sense to consider skin color (black or white) within the more profound context of body representation.

The "divided self" of the culture of alienation has been most radically split by man's progressive devaluation of his corporeality. The split between the body and a trans-substantial ego (disembodied) is considered here to have been the most radical of the splits in the endopsychic

14

structure of alienated man. The negation of man's corporeality assumed the character of a massive sociocultural dissociation. This issue is given attention in the next section. The body representation theoretical framework will be used in conjuction with the cumulative insights of depth psychology to study alienation from the body in racist societies, understood within the broader context of man's alienation in advanced cultures.[15] The dimension of alienation is discussed first in preparation for the discussion of the development of the body-world and socialization in racist communities.

NOTES

1. John Vorster, the South African prime minister at the time of writing.

2. Albert Camus, *The Myth of Sisyphus,* (London: Hamish Hamilton) 1955.

3. This will be recognized as a statement made by Franz Fanon during one of his more ambivalent moments. Fanon must have attached significance to this observation. It appears in two separate contexts: at the beginning and at the end of *Black Skin, White Masks.* Its importance appears to be obscure; as it is not clear whether Fanon was presenting a statement of value or not. If he was, one would object strongly to his position: The alienation of the black man under white racism is not something to be traded for the alienation of the racist ("white destiny"). The racist creates his own destiny and that of his victim primarily because of his ontological insecurity and alienation from the radical possibilities of his being. The black man should not experience himself as having a present or future investment in getting lost in whiteness as he searches for ontological security. The two can only meet in future if each reserves his freedom to search in whatever direction he chooses.

4. See, G. M. Hopkins: "No worst, there is none . . ." cited at the beginning of this text.

5. Some such as Professor Shockley of Stanford University, a Nobel Prize winner in physics abuse the distinction of recognition in one field for license to dabble in racist genetics. His success with his campaign so far is attributed wrongly to the principle of freedom in its broadest application. When an individual freedom impinges on the possible freedoms of a whole racial group, tyranny must be suspected.

15

Some who profess devotion to values of academic freedom have a secret admiration for this man's courage—a courage to express hate which is very close to their hearts but which, for hypocritical reasons, they are reluctant to acknowledge. They experience this man as a controversial extension of their own egos, daring to insult the black man beyond their wildest dreams.

6. Black consciousness old and new has always been challenged by those who have preferred to understand it as a kind of neo- or counter-racism against whites. A good, current example of this collective projection is represented by the white reaction to the development of black consciousness in South Africa. South African white liberals blamed its development on the ruling Nationalist Party and its racist policies, warning that it represented the dangerous emergence of counter-racism. Nationalists, for their part, thought they could make political gain by blaming the liberals for the disillusionment of blacks and their subsequent restlessness. The Afrikaner racist is loathe to share his distinction with anybody else, least of all, a black man. He expectedly resorts to high-handed and authoritarian solutions of a politically repressive nature.

7. In Southern Africa (South Africa, Rhodesia, Namibia, Mozambique and Angola), the ex-colonial powers of the world continue to reap the rewards of colonial, racist relationships between blacks and whites, now generated and supported through an international web of world capitalism. It is certainly more comfortable to believe that racial problems in these areas are "domestic problems" for any one who continues to thrive on what are described in foreign policy statements as "family" dissentions. To see the situation in these terms obscures one's appreciation of one's secret, sometimes even open, participation in the dehumanization of the black majorities of the subcontinent. The white minority governments and their constituencies are on the firing line of an international conspiracy against black people.

8. A number of standard texts on the body image are available to the reader interested in reviews of the area as a whole. The following selection documented fully in the reference section could be recommended: A.L. Benton: *Right-left Discrimination and Finger Localization;* M. Critchley: *The Parietal Lobes;* W.H. Gorman: *Body Image and the Image of the Brain;* S. Fisher and S.E. Cleveland: *Body Image and Personality;* P. Schilder: *The Image and Appearance of the Human Body;* F.C. Shontz: *Perceptual and Cognitive Aspects of Body Experience.* In the more philosophical tradition, see also: M. Merleau-Ponty: *The Phenomenology of Perception.*

9. Writing in the *American Sociological Review* (28,3,339-364) as late as 1963 Slater observed: "American psychologists as a group have never become entirely reconciled to the psyche's residence in the body,

and most works mention, 'biological drives' with the same dutiful haste generally accorded to the war of 1812 in elementary American History texts. It is no accident that psychoanalytic ideas did not really become popular in the United States until they had been Americanized by the neo-Freudians, who eliminated the instinctual and biological elements. This transformation undoubtedly sprang from the same discomfort with the body that has inundated the land with deodorants" (p. 339).

10. The belief is emphasized here that the body has an internal representation of its own. One of the first objects that the child relates to is its own body. Perhaps for this reason, the body is first experienced primarily as an object to be explored like all other objects prior to its psychic elaboration which develops into an internal representation (body image). The term body "representation" is preferred to that of body "image" since the former is more in accord with the general and still developing terminology of object relations and representation. The operational significance of the body's representation for the individual is demonstrated by the effects of the *postural schema* (internal representation of the body) on posture, direction and determination of locality beyond the limits of the body.

11. This finding is significant in that it suggests that body representation is subject to a certain developmental pattern. In younger amputees, the body's representation is still in the process of unfolding and consolidating and so is the total self-constellation. In adults, however, the amputation represents a catastrophic event that shatters a fully developed system and thus requires reparations and the emergence of a new constellation almost *de novo*.

12. An individual's implicit knowledge about his/her body is not limited to the postural elements but covers a wide range of aspects of functioning.

13. In *The Parietal Lobes* Critchley discussed the controversy which developed around the Gerstmann syndrome. Reference may also be made to the other standard sources referred to earlier. Gerstmann claimed that the syndrome consisted of the following signs: (1) finger agnosia, (2) right-left disorientation, (3) agraphia and (4) acalculia; and it was found in association with a circumscribed lesion with localizing diagnostic value.

14. E. H. Erikson in *Identity: Youth and Crisis* (1968) has singled out the sense of "sameness" and "continuity" as the central elements of personal identity.

15. It is the author's conviction that only a culture of alienation has the psychological fantasy (unconscious) structure for the socialization of the racist. In the present study, to say that advanced technological cultures are cultures of alienation does not imply a categorical, value of comparison.

17

CHAPTER II

Alienation: The Body and Racism

As suggested before, estrangement from the body is not limited to individual experience under pathological conditions but is a more general sociocultural manifestation. Alienation from the reality of the body can be understood as a collective alienation of man in industrial and technological societies. The condition of being alienated has attracted a great deal of attention from sociologists, literary men and philosophers of various persuasions. Although interesting, a review of such contributions would not be the most useful approach for the limited objectives of the present study. Rather a general formulation of alienation, taking account of the reality of the body, is approached through a critical discussion of a select, limited number of contributions in the psychiatric-psychological area.

The selection may be seen as arbitrary on both theoretical and ideological grounds, but it has been made to ensure that one thinks not only in individual psychological terms but also in terms of psychic processes which, in the nature of social reality, have become collective in the sense of the materialization of a public (societal) consciousness. Frankl, van den Berg and Neumann, among others, have found it necessary to move out of the confines of strict depth psychological theory into the realm of the sociocultural—from ego-object to the entire object world. It should be clear later that, although they converge on the level of the psychosocial, they each represent a different perspective. None of these writers could be identified as having concerned himself with the problem of alienation *per se,* but their various formulations converge on the theme of man's alienation. The focus in this discussion of alienation will be directed on the body and racism, the main concerns in the present study.

Vikton Frankl's (1965, 1967) *existential analysis* represents a good point of departure; a brief discussion follows of his philosophical anthropology, his formulations regarding the human condition. A survivor of Nazi brutality, Frankl has made original contributions to what is sometimes described as existential psychiatry. He has maintained that his existential analysis is not only an analysis of being in the ontological sense but also concerns itself with the *meaning* of existence. His view is that it is necessary to proceed along these lines because current theories of man are reductionistic and inadequate. Theories of man's nature which have arisen from Freudian psychoanalysis are characterized by Frankl as the "homeostasis" or "tension reduction" models of man, their primary limitation being that they have led to a two-dimensional characterization of man as psyche and soma.

Current views of man should be substituted or supplemented by a three-dimensional ontology integrating soma, psyche and spirit. The spiritual dimension is described as the "noetic" dimension in existential analysis to avoid the religious, mystical connotations of the word "spirit." Existential analysis is supported by three

20

philosophical assumptions. The first relates to man's *freedom of will.* The concept of freedom, like that of responsibility, is central to Frankl's thinking. His notion of freedom of will and responsibility represents a spirited negation of any kind of determinism—social, biological or psychological.

However, an admission is made by Frankl to the effect that an individual's freedom may be limited by psychological, sociological and/or biological conditions, but only within certain limits. This means that, for each individual, an ultimate freedom beyond any possible limitations is available. That ultimate freedom is, for Frankl, the individual's ability for self-transcendence; his ability to transcend his existential situation into the noetic dimension where he is better able to adopt a free-will attitude towards limitations to his freedom.

A second related assumption of existential analysis is described as the *will to meaning.* This notion is seen within the context of existential analysis as a more meaningful formulation than the Freudian "will to pleasure" or the Adlerian "will to power." Frankl contends that the characterization of man must move even beyond Maslow's conception of "self-actualization." Pleasure, power and self-actualization may not be ends in themselves. Man is poised towards meaning—toward living a life in which values are of paramount importance. Frankl (1967) describes this orientation:

> Once meaning orientation turns into meaning confrontation, that stage of maturation and development is reached in which freedom—that concept so much emphasized by existentialist philosophy—becomes responsibleness. Man is responsible for the fulfillment of the specific meaning of his personal life. But he is also responsible before something, be it society, or humanity, or mankind, or his own conscience (p. 12).

21

The last assumption concerns the *meaning of life*. The meaning of life may be experienced through a confrontation with values of different kinds. Life is rendered meaningful through "experiential values" (what we get from life); "creative values" (what we give to life) and "attitudinal values" (the stand we adopt towards an unalterable fate).

In Frankl's view, the conditions of modern life have made it increasingly difficult for man to confront meaning (life) in accordance with the various value categories referred to above. This failure to lead a meaningful existence has tended to lead to the emergence of a variety of neuroses described by Frankl as existential or *noögenic neuroses*.

Existential frustration, that frustration which arises out of an experience of helplessness in the face of a meaningless life arises out of an *existential vacuum* (lack of individually meaningful life task). The central idea running through the notions of the existential vacuum and the accompanying existential frustration is an emphasis on *existential estrangement,* a term that can be described as referring to *an alienated condition characterized by a marked deficiency in the experiencing and actualization of meaning (values).* It is important here to emphasize that existential frustration and noegenic neuroses are, in our view, expressive of a kind of alienation. This alienation arises out of man's abdication of his orientation towards experience and meaning; towards freedom of will and responsibility. Frankl uses the terminology of existential analysis to express this social reality. He also identifies a number of sociological conditions and symptoms which have a causal relationship with man's extrangement (Frankl, 1965, 1967). These may be presented briefly as follows:

1. Modern man has an "ephemeral" attitude towards life, an attitude that expresses itself as a tendency to live from day to day without much planning.
2. A second notable characteristic of life in modern societies is a fatalistic and nihilistic attitude towards life. Modern man experiences himself as though he were over-determined, having little or no control over the course of his life.
3. In mass society, man ceases to be an individual. He is pressured into collective modes of thinking and feeling.
4. The existence of collective patterns of thinking and feeling support the development of fanaticism in which the individuality of others is not recognized.

Although the term alienation is not specifically used as a central category in Frankl's existential analysis, implications relating to alienation clearly emerge in his notions of the existential vacuum and existential frustration. Man's estrangement, so Frankl believes, arises from his failure to give sufficient attention to his spiritual and experiential nature—that dimension in his being concerned with the experiencing and expressing of values. Put in another way, man is alienated in the world because of a psychosocial process of self-denunciation and diminution that results in a failure to recognize the fullness of his being as soma, psyche and spirit. Modern mass society with its virulent anti-individualism makes it difficult for the individual to stand out clearly, to transcend both his own limitations and those of society.

In the description and analysis of complex psychosocial phenomena, it is often difficult to identify cause and effect with any reasonable amount of certitude. Frankl (1967) does attempt to be specific about the sources of man's alienation:

And in actual fact all the four symptoms can be shown to derive from fear of and flight from freedom and responsibility; yet freedom and responsibility together make man a spiritual being (p. 121).

This is reminiscent of Fromm's (1941) more extended treatment of the theme of escape from freedom. Frankl goes on to argue that in the intellectual history of the West, man has been characterized as "nothing but," a view of man's being which can only be reductionistic in the extreme. Three main "-isms" have been used to define man's being: *biologism, sociologism* and *psychologism.* As Frankl sees it, man has been defined as "nothing but" a bundle of reflexes or drives, a biological animal, a psychic mechanism or the product of the socioeconomic environment. He sees unpromising features in the social organization of society which may lead to further alienation; notable among these are increased automation and the ever increasing potential for more leisure time.

It should be evident even from this brief, far from exhaustive discussion that Frankl has been concerned with forming a more realistic, adequate anthropology—an ontology encompassing the somatic, spiritual and psychological dimensions. It is as though Frankl were saying that available theories of man's being suffer from a comparable kind of incompleteness (reductionism) such as that characteristic of modern man's alienation—an atrophy in his being excluding the vital dimension of his spiritual nature.

The renowned Dutch psychiatrist, van den Berg, has contributed a number of provocative and stimulating statements that further the present consideration of alienation. The concerns and ideas most relevant for the study of alienation are fortunately now available in English translation (van den Berg, 1971a; 1971b). It was probably due to his interest in change, or more specifically, what he

24

describes as historical psychology, that he was led to the formulation of his theory of the social origin of the neuroses. The ideas supporting the development of this position are most useful in the theoretical study of the problem of alienation.

An idea of profound importance for the study of alienation is van den Berg's notion of *multiplicity* in the individual existence of man in industrial society. It appears to have been in pursuance of this idea, an attempt to determine its historical origins, that he developed his theory of the social origins of the neuroses. A strong conviction emerges from several of his writings that the neuroses, and by the same token, "life in multiplicity" were probably non-existent prior to the eighteenth century (van den Berg, 1971a, 1971b). In his view, the first important statement on the condition he describes as life in multiplicity (*leven in neervoud*) was that of William James in his *Principles of Psychology* published in 1891. James conceptualized the self as consisting of a material self, a spiritual self, and a social self; thus introducing the notion of multiple levels of interaction and organization of endopsychic structure.

James' *Principles of Psychology* was published in 1891. It was no coincidence, argues van den Berg, that at that time a list of publications appeared dealing with the idea of a divided self, a multiplicity in endopsychic structure. In 1886, R. L. Stevenson published his well known *Dr. Jekyll and Mr. Hyde,* while in 1888 F. W. van Eeden published a treatise on *Our Double Ego.* The year 1893 stands out as having been the most important because it was during that year that Freud and Breuer made their historic discovery of the unconscious. Also during the same year, the French sociologist Emile Durkheim published his classic on the division of labor (*De la Division du Travail Social*). Van den Berg (1971a) summarizes these developments in the following terms:

25

It seems justified to characterize the period around 1890 as years of particular interest for the duality or multiplicity of our existence, an assertion which suggests that the proximity of the publications by James and Durkheim is not at all a matter of accident. Both stem from a new pattern of life, which might have been in the making for a long time, but by then had become manifest (p. 399).

Indeed it is remarkable that it was at the time of James and Durkheim that the unconscious was discovered in the psychiatric patients of the time, and that at this time the double motif emerged as a literary format in Stevenson's novel.

Van den Berg's notion of multiplicity ought to be understood in both psychological and sociological terms. The notion of multiplicity in the psychological structure of the individual personality is not as strange and unfamiliar as it may appear at first sight. In depth psychology the concept of the conscious and unconscious is a recognition of duality in psychic organization. Some object-relation theorists even think in terms of a "multiplicity of egos" (Fairbairn, 1954). On the societal level, multiplicity arises from the condition Durkheim described as *anomie* (état de dérèglement). Van den Berg is of the view that anomie, the societal disorganization which created the social-psychological conditions for the development of the multiple existence, had its inception during the eighteenth century. The industrial revolution, a blessing in several important respects, created conditions that led to radical changes in the structure and organization of society. Under the anomic conditions first described by Durkheim, everyone has to contend with a multiplicity of roles, positions and tasks that are generally played out and acted on in the most diverse groups and situations. This state of affairs is described by van den Berg (1971a):

A condition of—literally—bondlessness. If the state of anomy exceeds a certain level, or in other words, if the grip

26

of the community as a whole has lost its strength on each of its individual members, this individual arrives in a condition of loneliness, of misfortune and despair, a condition which may induce him to commit suicide (p. 398).

In the consideration of the dynamic interaction between the individual and society, the dangers of social disorganization for the individual's psychic health become evident. What van den Berg establishes is the fact that a disorganized society creates an imbalance in the psychological life of individuals living in the society. This relationship between the individual and society has been described as follows by van den Berg (1971a):

> Not merely the happiness of man's existence, but also the clarity, the consciousness of it, is a consequence of the degree of homogeneity in society. If society is divided in some way or other, but ultimately is a unity, preferably a firm unity, then the individual is clear minded; with him, little or nothing is unconscious. If society is not a unity and hence fails to bind the individual unambiguously, then the individual will drop a portion of his existence, which means; he is not clear minded, anyway not completely so; there is in him an unconscious territory (pp. 400-401).

The implication of this position is that unity in individual psychic structure exists to the extent to which society is characterized by homogeneity in its social organization.

Convinced that neuroses are caused by sociological conditions, van den Berg has taken great pains to delineate the changes in the contents of the unconscious which have accompanied changes in the values and socioeconomic organization of society. He uses examples such as Anna O., the famous patient of Breuer's between 1880 and 1882, to show how the unconscious may function as an anti-ego; as a double in the self-system. In the case of Breuer's patient, her anti-ego or unconscious was dominated by repressed

27

sexuality and aggression. This split or duality in the consciousness of Anna O. was reflective of an equally dualistic split in the Vienna society of the time: the dichotomy between a life of virtue as against a life of sin (sexuality and aggression).

What emerges from van den Berg's analysis of change is a well-documented conviction that prior to the present century, the social repression of sexuality was responsible for a brand of patients such as Anna O. whose presenting symptoms were bodily. The release of sexuality from repression, which may be said to be in a sense characteristic of most societies today, has led to a notable change in the character of the unconscious of modern man. A new subtle and perversive denial and suppression has been set in motion: the denial of man's spirituality. The patients that consult the psychotherapist today rarely present with bodily symptoms; this can be illustrated with an excerpt from van den Berg (1971b):

"Can you tell me what brings you here?" asks the therapist.
". . . I can try," says the patient. "It is not easy and there is so much to tell I do not really know where to start. I have been thinking about my problems so much that now I feel quite dazed. How could I possibly tell you just like that what is wrong with me?"
"So you do not know where your difficulties lie?" the therapist asks.
"I do in a way," the patient replies, "but not exactly. I do know in any case what I consider important for myself. What has always been troubling me most, and still is, is that I find myself an insignificant little man. Yes, that is it. That is what I feel like. I can't stop feeling inferior."
"Do you feel that other people are always master of the situation?" the therapist asks.
"Yes," says the patient, "you could put it that way. However . . . everybody? Yes. Everybody always gets the better of me. I feel small. Of no significance." (p. 365).

In implicating industrial technological society for the conditions of social disorganization, van den Berg identifies himself with Karen Horney who believed that the neuroses of the present time arise because of contradictions in the value systems of Western societies. These contradictions, combined with the social condition of anomie, confront the individual with an existence characterized by "chaos."

Van den Berg's contribution and its implications with regard to alienation will be returned to. Before going further, however, Neumann's equally important ideas must be considered. Neumann was a Jungian analyst. The question relating to Neumann's use of the concept of the unconscious with respect to the collectivity is pertinent to the present discussion.

The way in which Neumann employs the concept of the unconscious with regard to the collectivity, what he characterizes as the "shadow side," approximates what one would generally describe as the *cultural unconscious*—a collectively available complex of impulses, affects and fantasies available to individuals sharing a specific sociocultural historicity. This signification of the term appears to be free from the notion of *archetypes* as constituents of a kind of given collective unconscious. In *Depth Psychology and a New Ethic,* Neumann is fairly inconsistent in his usage, sometimes moving close to the cultural unconscious notion and at other times slipping back to the Jungian universalistic conception. The former connotation is suggested, for example, in the following passage (1969):

This "rift," which in a more or less obvious form runs through the psyche of every modern person, occurs when the processes of differentiation which lead to the development of consciousness endanger the means of communication with the dark side of the unconscious. Man learns to identify himself as far as is possible with the ego as the centre of the conscious mind; he learns to comply with the ethical demands presented to him by the collective and to identify himself to a large extent with the light world of moral values and of consciousness, and at the same time to do his best to rid himself of the so-called "anti-values" by the techniques of suppression and repression.

Evidence of this "rift" in the psychic system is to be found in the fact that the split personality identifies itself with the powers of light, but leaves the powers of darkness (the shadow side) in projected form and then experiences and combats them in the shape of "the evil out there" (pp. 138-39).

Throughout his analysis of evil, Neumann emphasizes, as will be seen a little later, the role of absolutistic ethical demands which lead to suppression and repression, processes which create the shadow side in both the individual and the collective.

A departure from the conception of the cultural unconscious to a classical Jungian position is evident in several portions of the study. One such an example is the following passage which comes almost immediately before the passage quoted above:

At first, the figure of the shadow is experienced externally as alien and an enemy, but in the course of its progressive realization in consciousness it is introjected and recognized as a component of one's own personality. Yet when the personal shadow has been assimilated, the *archetypal shadow* (in the form of the Devil or Adversary) still remains potent in the psyche. This archetypal shadow-figure has a specific meaning for man as his antagonist in the process of development towards consciousness. The same insight—that the psychological basis for the phenomenon of the shadow is to be found in man's development towards consciousness—was formulated by Jung (p. 138).

The above observations have been made in order to clear the way for the view of the cultural (collective) unconscious which is used in this discussion of Neumann's contribution to the understanding of the condition of alienation. Although the implied distinction is conceptually important, it cannot adequately be dealt with in the present context.

In a century which has witnessed some of the most deadly wars in human history, it is not surprising for Neumann to have considered the problem of evil to be one of the most pressing issues of his time. He combined this concern with a broader interest in the development of consciousness both in the individual and the collective (Neumann, 1954, 1969, 1973). The ideas most relevant for the present study emerge mainly from his later work.

He approaches the problem of evil through a study of what he has described as the "old ethic" (Neumann, 1969). This ethic had its primary origins in the Judeao-Christian and Greek traditions. It is an "old ethic" to the extent that, it now lacks relevance for the complex ethical problems of man in the twentieth century; an indication that a new ethic should take sufficient account of man's unconscious or "shadow side."

The old ethic was based primarily on the ideal of human perfection. It was a dualistic ethic founded on an almost ritualistic distinction between good and evil, God and devil, purity and dirt, with an associated symbolism relating good to light and evil with darkness. The assumed opposition between good and evil was extended into an elaborate principle of "opposites in conflict" such as that between the soul (spirit) and flesh (body). This last distinction was probably responsible for the idea which defined man as having "higher" and "lower" faculties. In the light of these considerations, we should be in a better position to appreciate why the ideal figure for this ethic was always the *hero,* pure, perfect and good.

The old ethic, at the prime of its influence in Western societies, was absolutistic. The demands of this ethic were met through the processes of suppression and repression. Because of its absolutistic, dualistic and moralistic imperatives, its effects were not only detrimental to the psychic integrity of individuals but also created problems in the area of intergroup relationships. Neumann saw the source of intergroup tensions as the development in the personality of Western man of a split between the conscious and unconscious spheres of consciousness. He relates this split to the demands of the old ethic in the following terms (1969):

> We have seen that suppression and repression are the two main techniques employed by the individual in his attempt to achieve adaptation to the ethical ideal. The natural result of this attempt is the formation of two psychic systems in the personality, one which usually remains completely unconscious, while the other develops into an essential organ of the psyche, with the active support of the ego and conscious mind. The system which generally remains unconscious is the shadow: the other system is the "facade personality" or persona (p. 37).

Neumann has argued that the cultural unconscious developed out of the categorical distinction between "inferior corporeality" and a belief in the absoluteness of the human spirit that was characteristic of the old ethic. The unconscious became, under conditions governing the old ethic, the repository of all the bodily appetites that were rejected by society. It is this rejected portion of the individual and social existence which creates tensions not only in the individual but also in the life of whole groups and nations. The tensions which arise from this massive

32

collective repression are resolved through the process of projection which, in the case of the collective, sometimes leads to scapegoating.

In Neumann's mind (1969), there was no question about the fact that the problem of the scapegoat, be it the Jew, Negro or Protestant, could be accounted for on the basis of the split in the consciousness of groups and its resolution through the mechanism of projection:

> This psychological problem of the minorities is to be found with religious, national, racial and social variations; it is, however, symptomatic, in every case, of a split in the structure of the collective psyche. . . . In the economy of the psyche, the outcast role of the alien is immensely important as an object for the projection of the shadow. The shadow—that part of our personality which is "alien" to the ego, our own unconscious counterposition, which is subversive of our conscious attitude and security—can be exteriorized and subsequently destroyed (p. 52).

Adherence to the prescriptions of the old ethic required, for the expansion of the ego sphere and the values that were cherished at the time, greater degrees of suppression and repression. The old ethic was a partial ethic; partisan to the inflation of the ego at the expense of the unconscious. Man's estrangement developed from an ethical attitude that encouraged a one-sided view of psychic reality. Alienation may be seen, therefore, as the price man has to pay for an incomplete recognition of his nature.

The effects of a dualistic world view on society and individuals were a concern of Neumann's for a number of years. Late in the development of his thinking, he became more articulate about what he saw as a dualistic world view and the polarization of the body into an upper and lower pole, another expression of this duality. How the devaluation and polarization of the body evolved in society and in individual development will be seen later.

33

The problems created by man's dualistic psychic organization are not to be solved by the unrealistic elimination of the unconscious as a psychological reality. The solution would appear to demand the development of a new ethic and a new attitude towards reality characterized, *inter alia*, by an equal recognition of man's somatic and spiritual qualities. On the basis of such an integrative approach—the acceptance of both corporeality and spirituality—man's consciousness can be further expanded and enriched.

Starting then with Frankl the collective neuroses of the present century reflect an endemic fear of freedom and responsibility, it follows that, man's sense of psychosocial dislocation—his alienation—develops out of his failure to achieve wholeness. This condition of incompleteness is expressed in practice as a failure to confront meaning by actualizing values. In spite of his emphasis on man's wholeness as a three-dimensional being, Frankl's position on man's estrangement is markedly sociocultural. It differs in important respects from the more psychodynamic approaches of thinkers such as Herbert Marcuse.

While Frankl hardly discusses repression and the unconscious, Marcuse considers that the "repressive civilization" of the West should be replaced by a "non-repressive" one. In Marcuse's discussion of Freud's analysis of the development of Western civilization, the problem of alienation is related directly to the process of repression. Repression, however, is no longer in the service of the reality principle as formulated by Freud but serves what Marcuse (1955) describes as the "performance principle":

> The conflict between sexuality and civilization unfolds with this development of domination. Under the rule of the performance principle, body and mind are made into instruments of alienated labor; they can function as such instruments only if they renounce the freedom of the libidinal

subject-object which the human organism primarily is and desires (p. 42).

Later he observes:

> The preceding analysis tried to identify certain basic trends in the instinctual structure of civilization and, particularly, to define the specific reality principle which has governed the progress of Western civilization. We designated this reality principle as the performance principle; and we attempted to show that domination and alienation, derived from the prevalent social organization of labor, determined to a large extent the demands imposed upon the instincts by this reality principle (p. 117).

The demands on the instincts naturally refers to the demands on individuals in society. Following Freud's identification of civilization with repression (the ascendency of the reality principle), Marcuse also regards repression as the central dynamic in the progressive alienation of industrial man.

Frankl fails to point out that even when it has been recognized that man is a somatopsychic unity, sufficient attention still has not been given to the psychological reality of the body. It is indeed true to say that psychologists continue to indulge in a psychologism, which gives the body the status of a spurious reality. In this psychism, psychologists have stayed very close to the popular societal attitudes and feelings relating to the human body. One of the primary thrusts towards progress in science and technology has been and is the mastery of man's environment. It is indeed unfortunate that this orientation towards mastery of nature also included the human body as one of its main targets. Body-related desires such as sexuality became the victims of massive social control in the interests of human progress.[1] This suppression of the bodily demanded for its effectiveness a concurrent devaluation of the body.

What is popularly described as progress has been achieved at the expense of the wholeness or totality of man's experience of his being. The failure to recognize man's multi-dimensional nature, which characterizes the state of alienation, is supported by a conception of man which is essentially uni-dimensional. This notion of man has placed dramatic emphasis on the ego's unlimited potential for expansion.

The danger of the anthropological corrective Frankl wishes to introduce arises from a possible reluctance on man's part to recognize that disalienation will not occur the moment man begins to confront meaning but when body, psyche and spirit are recognized and integrated into an expanded and richer consciousness. While this is not sufficiently recognized, meaning confrontation will be nothing more than a misguided trend towards the splitting of human consciousness. In general, the study of the neuroses invariably seems to lead to the problem of man's alienation. In addition, the study of the neuroses involves questions about the mechanism of repression. Van den Berg's contribution to the theory of the neuroses provides evidence supporting these observations. He places a great deal of emphasis on the effects on the individual of social disorganization or anomie. Anomie creates multiplicity in endopsychic structure, part of which becomes repressed and returns in one form of neurosis or another. In more recent times, the targets of social suppression have changed. In many societies, sexuality has been released from societal suppression with abandon. It is still too early to tell whether this "new" attitude towards sexuality is reflective of changing attitudes towards the body or is a societal over-compensation for a shrinking capacity for experience at the spiritual level.

That this may well be the case is suggested by van den Berg's observation that the spiritual dimension is modern man's new victim—the subject of societal denial and suppression. This change expresses itself in new kinds of patients who are not neurotic in the classical sense. In a statement that refers to Frankl, van den Berg (1971b) comments on these developments in the following way:

> He who suffered from the disease of the old white sector (repressed sexuality and aggression), suffered from his body as it were—the symptoms that emerged were physical. The patient had palpitations, a disturbed sight, even a paralyzed arm, as in the case of Anna O. But whoever is suffering from the sector spirituality, is free from bodily complaints. He is only unhappy. He is characterized by a mild, friendly sort of unhappiness. He knows no simple joys in life. And yet, is the world not wonderful? Is the world not full of meaning in all its manifestations (p. 355)? [parentheses added.]

This last statement reminds us of Guntrip's (1971) description of the "schizoid condition." The similarities between this condition and the kind of patient van den Berg discusses are more than sheer coincidence. Guntrip emphasizes the fact that the schizoid condition is not a "fixed entity" but a core condition which may be found in association with a number of other psychopathological trends. The condition of inner isolation—the experience of a feeling of futility (often described as depression) and a lack of certainty about one's identity—are features characteristic of the schizoid condition. Observing that the problem of man's alienation is a growing concern of sociologists, he goes further to suggest that psychodynamic research must lead the way to the real roots of the problem. The roots of the problem of alienation, of which the schizoid condition is only one of its manifestations, must be sought not only in sociocultural conditions but in the early and significant experiences of individuals in the mother-child relationship. The mother-child relationship is taken up more fully in a later section. In various ways and in different contexts, the study of the origins of the neuroses tends to lead to the crucial problem of alienation in general. What has traditionally been a sociological and more recently a philosophical and literary problem has emerged as one of the most important problems for the psychological sciences.

Neumann was convinced that the central problem of modern man is the split in his psychic organization—the split between ego and the unconscious. To the extent that the demands of the old ethic were partial to an obsessional perfectionist orientation, they fostered suppression and repression to the detriment of the individual and the collective. Two important points emerge from Neumann's formulation of the problem of evil: the first is that a dualistic ethical attitude did not only lead to a dualistic *weltanschuung* but also created an identical dualism in man's consciousness of his being; the second point is that man developed in the progress of civilization a dualistic and polarized conception and experience of his body.

To understand and delineate the psychosocial devaluation of the body in the progress of Western civilization, this denial of the bodily must be placed within a more inclusive framework, namely that of alienated man in society. The route adopted for effecting this approach has been to consider a number of theoretical psychological contributions which have a bearing on alienation. Through this analysis, it has been intended to demonstrate the fact that any serious and thoughtful statement on the human condition during this and preceding centuries will invariably throw the problem of alienation into prominence. Differences in approaches to the problem do not appear to be of particular significance since authors tend to agree on the primary source of man's sense of psychosocial dislocation.

The core condition, identified as the most important regarding the problem of alienation, is the process of psychic splitting that results from the need for repression. The first, most crucial development that created conditions favorable to the process of psychic splitting was the ascendency of the dualistic Judaeo-Christian ethic. After the industrial revolution and the subsequent phenomenal rise of an industrial-technological culture, the general effects of the old ethic on man's social organization were consolidated by the new demands of the "performance principle." The ideals of individuals and nations made a progressive shift from concerns about eternal life to what can be described as the "from rags to riches" orientation—an orientation committed to work and progress. The impact of these developments on modern man have been the subject of searching scrutiny by Brown (1959; 1966), Marcuse (1955), Fromm (1941), and Kovel (1970).

The split in man's experience of his being, most important in this study, is that associated with the societal devaluation of the body. Throughout man's history, the body has been the object of disturbing ambivalence. It has always been real or substantial enough for it not to be ignored completely. But under the conditions of the old ethic—which is generally still operative—the body has been experienced as an object that could stand in man's way to eternal life. It was identified with weakness and sin and seen as the devil incarnate. At the same time the body was surreptitiously alluded to as "God's temple" and not to be defiled. The attitude of suspicion towards everything that was bodily—sexual desire, excrement, menstrual blood and the feelings which accompany sexual desire—was undermined only by gratification on the sly. The class of people in Western society to have been victimized more than any other group by this ambivalence towards the body were women. Stereotypes were developed to go with this ambivalence such as the one that said that woman was all emotion and no thought. Indeed, women psychologists may begin to provide interesting and important data on this development.

What society denied or suppressed was not primarily sexuality *per se*. The denial of sexuality and its repression by individuals, such as those discussed by van den Berg, was expressive of a more inclusive rejection of corporeality in favor of a promised eternal life of bliss. The initial denial of the bodily was further consolidated by developments that placed a high premium on progress, reason and the mastery of the human environment. This mastery required the mastery of bodily appetites, including sexuality. Two broad historical movements—the old ethic (mainly its religions) and the scientific and industrial revolutions—created the conditions for the split in man's psyche. The vital bodily sphere was dropped from active awareness and the ego sphere was expanded at its expense.

Among the writers who have attempted to understand large scale sociocultural phenomena using a social-psychological framework is Wilhelm Reich. His *The Mass Psychology of Fascism.* (1970), among other things, is a repudiation of Marxist ideologists who have attempted to account for mass phenomena such as fascism on a socio-economic basis. He considers socio-economic explanations inadequate simply because they consistently fail to bring into account the "subjective factor" in human affairs. An adequate account is achievable only in a multilevel conceptualization combining both social reality and the character structure of man. As Reich understood it, man's character structure consisted of three levels or layers: an outer surface layer of social cooperation, a secondary unconscious (identified with Freudianism) and a biologic core considered as the deepest layer. His belief that man's most excruciating problems, such as fascism and racism, are to be understood on the basis of a tragic and radical split in the given nature of his character structure is both explicit and consistent with the view of alienation being developed in this study. Reich observes (1970):

> There would be no social tragedy of the human animal if this surface layer of the personality were in direct contact with the deep natural core (p. xi).

He contested the Freudian position which identifies sexual suppression and repression with the progress of Western civilization and culture:

> The question, then, is no longer one relating to culture, but one relating to social order. If one studies the history of sexual repression, one finds that it cannot be traced back to the beginnings of cultural development; suppression and repression, in other words, are not the presuppositions of cultural development. It was not until relatively late, with the establishment of an authoritarian patriarchy and the beginning of the division of the classes, that suppression of sexuality begins to make its appearance. It is at this stage that sexual interests in general begin to enter the service of a minority interest in material profit; in the patriarchal marriage and family this state of affairs assumes a solid organizational form. With the restriction and suppression of sexuality, the nature of human feelings changes; a sex-negating religion comes into being and gradually develops its own sex-political organization, the church with all its predecessors, the aim of which is nothing other than the eradication of man's sexual desires and consequently of what little happiness there is on earth. There is good reason for all this when seen from the perspective of the now-thriving exploitation of human labor (p. 29).

41

Towards the end of his study of fascism, Reich makes it very clear that underlying all human ideology is a frantic denial of man's biologic (animal) nature and his sexuality:

> "Away from the animal; away from sexuality!" are the guiding principles of the formation of all human ideology. This is the case whether it is disguised in the fascist form of racially pure "supermen," the communist form of proletarian class honor, the christian form of man's "spiritual and ethical nature," or the liberal form of "higher human values." All these harp on the same monotonous tune: "We are not animals; it was we who discovered the machine—not the animal! And *we* don't have genitals like the animals!" All this adds up to an overemphasis of the intellect, of the "purely" mechanistic; logic and reason as opposed to instinct; culture as opposed to sexuality; the state as opposed to the individuals; the superior man as opposed to the inferior man (p. 339).

Reich, like Marcuse, Neumann, van den Berg and Freud, recognized the significance for man's condition of the processes of suppression and repression. Reich, like Neumann, arrives at a position that is in accord with the position taken in the present study with respect to the social-historical tribulations of the human body in the development of human consciousness.

What could be more animal in man's nature than his corporeality! To deny, suppress or repress sexuality is to negate the vital biologic core of man's nature. Within the context of Reich's thinking, the denial of the biological core can be seen to create a kind of incompleteness in man's experience of his being—a transformation, which combined with soicocultural conditions, erupts into various dramatic forms of alienation such as fascism and the variations of racism which have characterized the relations of racial groups throughout the history of man.

A strong impression developed thus far is that man's devaluation of his body accompanied his socioeconomic progress which is at the root of his experience of a lack of wholeness and unity. The alienated consciousness which flourished under these conditions is always polarized. It represents not only a dualistic experience of its being (soma and psyche), but of all of reality. Body and soul, heaven and earth, us and them: these polarizations add up to the most tragic polarizations, namely that between the ego sphere and the unconscious. Mainly because of this polarized consciousness, even the growing child is socialized to absorb these polarizations. The child is socialized to distinguish between "good objects" and "bad objects," between self and non-self and between "good body" and "bad body."

After two world wars and the ever imminent possibility of a third one, Frankl's concern about the sphere of values and Neumann's focus on evil are understandable. But man's earlier concern about the spiritual was disastrous because it was achieved at the cost of psychic wholeness and unity. With the secularization of life in modern cultures, the risk of the negation of man's spirituality is very real. But here again, the focus of espoused solutions to the problem of alienation should not be partial to any of the three spheres of man's being. The most general proposition which can be made is that whatever path man chooses to follow he should safeguard against the process of splitting his consciousness.

After recognizing society's active negation of man's corporeality, it is now possible to move to a variety of alienation characteristic of race supremacist cultures. Inasmuch as racism dehumanizes both the racist and his victim, it represents a variation of the condition of being alienated. The healthy state of affairs is the existential counter-reality; the flip side of alienation. The primary features of the unalienated state are easily identified though difficult to actualize in real life situations.

Wholeness and unity are the most important attributes of the authentic condition. Authenticity is a potential to be actualized only when the multidimensional nature of man is recognized and integrated. To insist on an integration of the soma, the psyche and the spiritual dimension is not enough; it is necessary to proceed beyond this notion and make additional observations. A useful approach to the question of authenticity as wholeness and unity is to recognize man as a being in-the-world. There is a structure to man's situatedness in the world which may be described briefly as follows.

The first feature of man's situatedness in the world has to do with a constant dialogue (relating), primarily at four different but equally important levels or spheres. The individual establishes relations first with his body. The body is for the individual, the first and primary reality or gestalt that presents itself as a totality to be experienced. The second sphere of interaction consists of the interpersonal relationships established by the individual as he or she develops. The "other" of the interpersonal relationship may consist of what Frankl (1965) describes as "suprameaning": some meaning beyond man's earthly life. Thirdly man establishes and relates to culture. He relates to things and objects. Finally, time and space, in the individual existence, are as real as the body. Within this analytical framework, authenticity as wholeness and unity exists whenever an individual is fully in touch with these various spheres of his existential configuration.

The march of Western civilization made it very difficult for individuals to be vital and real in their transactions with their bodies. Society coerced its members into an uncomfortable denunciation of the bodily as a necessary sacrifice for the achievement of an unprecedented material prosperity. This development led to the already noted splitting of human consciousness into an overexaggerated ego stream alienated from the unconscious sphere. What this analysis of alienation has shown, is that once society compels its members to lose touch with any of the spheres of the existential structure, individuals lose their sense and experience of wholeness and unity. In addition, a process of psychic internal polarization develops, making a significant portion of his existence unavailable to him. For authenticity to occur, the various existential spheres of interaction (body, others, objects and things, space and time) must, at most times, be equally available to the individual. When this condition is not met, a state of incompleteness, a kind of prematurity, sets in. Alienation may then be seen as a state of incompleteness in self-consciousness.

By identifying the condition of alienation with the progress of Western civilization, the analysis has been moving cautiously towards the position that alienation is a price man in industrialized societies has had to pay for his material prosperity. It is a condition which developed as a result of a complex network of historical developments; developments in which the man of color had no active participation. This does not mean that the black man is free from alienation. If he is a citizen of a highly industrialized country, the chances are that he is alienated on two counts. One variety of alienation is a condition which he shares with his white counterpart. It is the second variety of alienation, a variety which the man of color has shared with the Jew, among others, which requires scrutiny. This condition arose with the historical development of what, following Sartre (1948), will be described as "situations." For purposes of analysis, it is possible to discuss the *situation of the racist* as opposed to the *situation of the victim of racism.*[2] The condition of alienation or dehumanization which accompanied the

45

evolution of these situations will be the main concern for the rest of this section.

Two important contributions on the situations of the victim of racism have been made by Sartre (1948) and Fanon (1967). The distinction between the alienation of the racist, one which he shares with the rest of the industrialized societies of the world, and the alienation suffered by the victim of racism may be formulated in the following terms. The racist belongs to the class of "absurd" man; he suffers from existential frustration and a sense of helplessness. The victim, be he Jew or African, has not achieved the status of the absurd man. There will always be exceptions, but these are not the most important element in the situation. The absurd man status is hardly available to the victim because his situation is predominantly *social* in the Sartrian sense. This is another way of saying that, for the black or the Jew, getting into the world, which means being defined in terms other than Jewishness or blackness, is a very difficult task (Sartre, 1948).

> The disquietude of the Jew is not metaphysical; it is social. The ordinary object of his concern is not yet the place of man in the universe, but his place in society. He cannot perceive the loneliness of each man in the midst of a silent universe, because he has not yet emerged from society into the world. It is among men that he feels himself lonely; the racial problem limits his horizon. Nor is his uneasiness of the kind that seeks perpetuation; he takes no pleasure in it—he seeks reassurance. . . .
>
> It is society, not the decree of God, that has made him a Jew and brought the Jewish problem into being. As he is forced to make his choices within the perspective set by this problem, it is in and through the social that he chooses even his own existence. His constructive effort to integrate himself in the national community is social; social is the effort he makes to think of himself, that is, to situate himself, among

46

other men; his joys and sorrows are social; but all this is because the curse that rests upon him is social. If in consequence he is reproached for his metaphysical inauthenticity, if attention is called to the fact that his constant uneasiness is accompanied by a radical positivism, let us not forget that these reproaches return upon those who make them: the Jew is social because the anti-Semite has made him so (pp. 134-35).

The victim of racism suffers from a primary deficit: that of being overly socialized. He is over-determined from inside and outside. "The absurd man projected by Camus directs his question (the 'why') to existence (life), as it were, or perhaps to God. The black man, on the other hand, directs his question to life as imposed on him by the white man (Manganyi, 1973, p. 47).[3] The white man—who may be a racist if he should be a South African, a Rhodesian or for that matter, a European or American—indulges himself with metaphysical questions. He would make a good candidate for Frankl's logotherapy, a kind of therapy that has its primary focus on the meaning of life.[4]

The situations of the racist and his victim(s) are characterized by different types of inauthenticity. In both situations, however, inauthenticity invades individuals at any one of the spheres of interaction described above. Sartre and Fanon have explored, in depth, the psychological elements that constitute alienation in the different situations. However, they have not paid adequate attention to experiencing the body-world in the two situations. Sartre, for one, dismissed the issue with a passing reference.

The anti-Semite is concerned with the Jew's personality as a whole, Sartre argues; and makes the following additional observations (1948):

There is a disgust for the Jew, just as there is a disgust for the Chinese or the Negro among certain people. Thus it is not

47

from the body that the sense of repulsion arises, since one may love a Jewess very well if one does not know what her race is, rather it is something which enters the body from the mind (p. 11).

That "something which enters the body from the mind" leads to stereotyping. Because of the process of stereotyping which accompanied the evolution of anti-Semitism, the Jew has ended up with problems relating to his body.

Sartre suggests that the problems experienced by the Jew regarding his body probably arise from his attempt to escape his Jewishness. The body must be denied—a collusion with the anti-Semite who has always professed an ability to identify the Jew on sight. But this denial is not simple because it is achieved at a complex psychological level. The Jew conceives of his body as a "universal and rationalized" body, thus he is able to treat his body as though it were merely an instrument. In contrast, the Aryan developed an "aristocracy of the body." Sartre is quick to point out that the values linked with this idealized conception of the body are also related to "anti-values," which express a devaluative attitude towards the so-called "lower functions" of the body.

He supports the view adopted in this analysis, that the progress of Western civilization was accompanied by a denegation of the body and its functions. The Aryan, the epitome of Christian and cultural values, pre-empted the vital values not only from his own body but particularly from the bodies of non-Aryans. In Sartre's characterization of the "aristocracy" of the Aryan body can be seen some of the most compelling arguments for the fact that the Aryan body was deodorized even before the arm-pit industry began to flourish. Deodorants are the most recent physicalization of values which have always supported the centuries old myth of the Aryan body. It should be remembered that the Aryan indulged in the most grandiose self-deceptions regarding the reality of his relations with his body. The attempt to abandon the bodily in favor of "higher functions" was in itself unachievable. One of the solutions, in addition to scapegoating involved a compensatory development of an almost ethereal *sociological (normative) schema* of his body. The ethereal quality of this schema is noticeable in the following statement (Sartre, 1948):

> *He does not have a pure and simple consciousness of the massive modifications of his organs; the messages and appeals that his body sends him come with certain coefficients of ideality, and are always more or less symbolic of vital values. He even devotes a portion of his activity to procuring perceptions of himself that correspond to his vital ideal* (p. 120). (Italics added).

The Aryan's consciousness or experience of his body could not be "pure" or "simple" since his consciousness would constitute a deviation from his ego and abstract orientation. Pure and simple consciousness of one's body requires an integration and recognition of the body's lower functions: sexuality, excreta and menstrual blood. These bodily realities are generally dissonant with grace and nobility. All the indications are, therefore, that the alienated man of the West, whose inauthenticity expressed itself as a polarization of his body experience, developed an elaborate compensatory *body aesthetic* to devour through awareness all elements of sexuality, bodily appetites and functions which were seen as being opposed to this body aesthetic.

The anti-Semite works himself up to the belief that he can recognize the Jew even if he were blindfolded since he need only smell him. This is passion. The Negrophobe such as Betsie Verwoerd, widow of one of South Africa's arch-architects of the racist *apartheid* machine,[5] like the anti-

49

Semite, may claim that she can smell an African as he takes a corner. She also suffers from an abundance of passion. Once the blindfolds are taken off and the corner turned, and the Jew and the African are exposed, one critical element emerges: the African places himself in immediate focus. He is the moving target (Fanon, 1967).

> The Negro's *sui generis* odor . . . the Negro's *sui generis* good nature . . . the Negro's *sui generis* gullibility . . . (p. 129).

In the situation of the Jew, problems involving the Jew's experience of his body were created by the Aryan and his alienation from his own body. The situation of the black man and his experience of his body raises problems of a different order of complexity. Detailed consideration is given to this complexity in the next chapter which covers the development of the child and its body-world.

It is necessary to move beyond the intellectually indolent attitude of thinking about the body either in terms of its epidermal or physioanatomical reality. In the section on "the fact of blackness," possibly one of the most profound and powerful Fanon ever wrote, he recognizes the dimensional character of the reality of the body. First, he suggests, as the author has elsewhere (Manganyi, 1973), that the black man encounters serious limitations in the development of his body image. The body image, as suggested earlier, is the individual's mental representation of his body in its totality. Fanon (1967) describes this image as follows:

> And all these movements were made not out of habit but out of *implicit knowledge.* A slow composition of myself as a body in the middle of a spatial and temporal world—such seems to be the schema. It does not impose itself on me; it is rather, a definitive structuring of the self and of the world— definitive because it creates a real dialectic between my body and the world (p. 111). [Italics added].

50

The body image or schema, *the primary body reality,* is the vital and core body reality; it develops, as will be shown later, from the integration of sensory experience: visual, tactile, kinesthetic and postural. Like the self-system as a whole, the body image shares the character of uniqueness and complexity. Fanon identified and described a "racial epidermal schema," which pre-empts the vitality of the body image or corporeal schema and which is described by the author as the *sociological schema.*

In later discussion, it will be shown that the corporeal schema and the sociological schema of the body develop and interact during individuation. The notion of the sociological schema actually goes beyond that of the racial epidermal schema. For example, it maintains that the Aryan aristocracy of the body is an overvalued mythological stereotype which had psychosocial origins. From this development, the notions of the "good" and "bad" bodies originated. This sociological schema, which was supported during its development by a body aesthetic, thrived and still thrives on its prescribed and assumed *appeal* features. In his contact with the Jew, the Aryan counterbalanced this meticulously sculptured body aesthetic and schema against a negative sociological schema of the Jewish body with all the body anti-values. The slave owner and the colonist did the same in their contact with Africans. The sociological schema of the body of the victim of racism is characterized by *barrier* or *distancing* features.

After this analysis, it is possible to arrive at the following formulation: Man in industrial societies has been invaded by a sense of estrangement from the reality of his being which may be understood and described in psychosocial terms. This estrangement results from self-inflicted amputations, the earliest of which involved the sphere of man's relations with the bodily. The vitality of the body was abandoned to the unconscious stream. In an attempt to rescue what remains of that lost vitality, modern man has taken another big leap towards effecting another fatal amputation: the denial of the reality of the sphere of spiritual values. In the light of these developments it is not surprising when this alienated man became an anti-Semite and/or Negrophobe. What was achieved was the global spread of an epidemic. The colonizer infected every African contacted with his own alienation. The Aryan infected the Jew, while the slave owner of America's plantations infected his slaves. A new kind of inauthenticity, a new kind of ontological dislocation was created in man's relations with his body, with others, and with objects, and with space and time. The world has not recovered from this dislocation. Where an industrial society is beginning to reach maturity, the dislocations are currently at their highest. Such is the case in South Africa, for example, where racism is flourishing alongside a booming economy.

The body was devalued and sacrificed in the development of Western civilization. The white man alienated himself from the reality of his body and worked progressively harder to compensate for the psychological tension created by this state of affairs by developing a compensatory body aesthetic and sociological schema of the body. The victim of racism became estranged from his body by contagion, so to speak. His devaluation of his body was primarily an external affair, and he accepted a body aesthetic that was not only dissonant with his body type, if he were Negroid; but most difficult, he accepted one which was actually unattainable.

1. Sexuality is identified in the history of Western civilization as the primary area of social suppression and individual repression, perhaps as a result of Freud's often misrepresented emphasis on sexuality. As a result and in addition to more complex reasons, writers on civilization and alienation fail to emphasize the negation of the body as a whole, sexuality included. This is the merit of Neumann and Reich who are explicit in this regard. To identify sexuality is to isolate the most concrete element in a highly mystified psychosocial reality.

2. The concept of *situation* is important for the understanding of racism of whatever variety. In *Anti-Semite and Jew*, Sartre clarifies the significance of this concept as follows: "What is it, then, that serves to keep a semblance of unity in the Jewish community? To reply to this question, we must come back to the idea of situation. It is neither their past, their religion, nor their soil that unites the sons of Israel. If they have a common bond, if all of them deserve the name of Jew, it is because they have in common the situation of a Jew, that is, they live in a community which takes them for Jews" (p. 67). Likewise, the African or the Afro-American lives in a world which takes him for a "nigger" or a "kaffir" while he believes himself to be simply a black man. The black man is inassimilable. In South Africa, for example, Africans who have the situation common to blacks are seen as a very real threat to whites even at the peak of political disarray. Again Sartre, strikes the nail on the head when he observes: "It is therefore the idea of the Jew that one forms for himself which would seem to determine history, not the 'historical fact' that produces the idea" (p. 16). The idea is very powerful. The idea of the African obstructs the rational formulation, understanding and solution of race problems in Southern Africa. It is also the idea of the African which makes the South African problem a generation problem—a problem assumed by those in power to require *ad hoc* measures for the benefit of the present generation of whites. After us the deluge!

3. In his essay, "The Rebel" (1955) Albert Camus extends his vision beyond the absurd: "Therefore, if it was legitimate to take absurdist sensibility into account, to make a diagnosis of a malady to be found in ourselves and in others, it is nevertheless impossible to see in this sensibility, and in the nihilism it presupposes, anything but a point of departure, a criticism brought to life—the equivalent, in the plane of existence, of systematic doubt. After this, the mirror, with its fixed stare, must be broken and we are, perforce, caught up in the irresistable movement by which the absurd exceeds itself" (pp. 9-10). Social man, the man who is over-determined by racism, has no good reasons for embracing the absurd sensibility of his "master." He can, as soon as the rebelious impulse

invades him move in leaps and bounds beyond the absurd. This should be possible once Camus' position is accepted that: "It is for the sake of everyone in the world that the slave asserts himself when he comes to the conclusion that a command has infringed on something in him which does not belong to him alone, but which is common ground where all men--even the man who insults and oppresses him—have a natural community." (p. 16)

4. Logotherapy is not intended as a replacement for psychoanalysis or psychotherapy in the generic sense of the word. It is one of the existential therapies focused primarily on meaning. Its main tool is what Frankl describes as "paradoxical intention." In the most classical situations, the patient is socialized in therapy to consciously (willfully) exploit his neurosis to the full. In the case of an obsession, for example, the patient could be encouraged to activate his obsession to absurdity such that he even begins to experience it as comical—an effect which creates distance between the patient and his illness. Very often, it is reported that the patient is unable to activate his illness when he tries under the controlled atmosphere of therapy.

5. Apartheid is the policy of racial discrimination and segregation against the black majority in South Africa. The term has lost its initial attraction for the ruling Afrikaner oligarchy and has since been substituted by the term "Separate Development"—a clumsy euphemism for racism.

CHAPTER III

The Body-World and the Ontogenesis of Racism

Exploratory studies of the body image using black South African samples and a careful study of the literature on the body image and racism constituted the germinal stages of the present analysis (Manganyi, 1972; Manganyi, Kromberg & Jenkins, 1974). An idea emerged in the course of time that has matured into the ideas presented in this section; an impression developed that racism, which in analysis must be distinguished from strategies for social change, requires a psychosocial context for adequate formulation. That, of course, is what Kovel (1970) did in his psychohistory of American white racism. Racism becomes understandable within the context of the alienation from the body both in the historical development of society and in the process of individuation. This approach offers promise for understanding the collective unconscious (cultural unconscious) and its effects on the manifest structure of social organization involved in institutionalized racism.

This approach offers unqualified support for Fisher (1973) who has observed:

> I think we will fail in our efforts to eradicate racist behavior until we cope with the irrational body anxiety that feeds it (p. 84).

The role of body experience during child development and its relationship with the ontogenesis of racist behavior has not yet been clearly articulated except in psychodynamic terms. In fact, although the systematic study and theoretical formulation of the child's progressive experience of its bodily self appears to be of such importance, it is remarkable that it has been grossly neglected in child development literature. Within this context the present analysis is seen as one which could help fill the need for the formulation of a developmental position, integrating body related concepts with those of the self-system as a whole. A second aim will be to present a set of theoretical propositions to account for the development of racist behavior during early body experience and socialization.

The psychodynamics of racism represent the scapegoat psychology par excellence. Racism, manifesting itself as anti-Semitism or prejudice against blacks, is the most complex and, in some instances such as in South African society, the most institutionalized kind of psychological scapegoating. Only recently has man begun to move from viewing racism in more than simple, rational sociopolitical terms.[1] This transition should be attributed to Freud for his general psychodynamic discoveries and to later, better appreciation of the fact that culture and civilization are the materialization of complex collective unconscious processes. The most articulate recognition of this relationship has come from the statements of Norman O. Brown (1959, 1966) and Herbert Marcuse (1955). In the light of this legacy of psychoanalysis, some workers, such as Kovel (1970), have found the notions of *anality* and the *Oedipal situation* useful in the exploration of the fantasies that accompany the process of scapegoating in race supremacist cultures. The present analysis should show that the dynamic relationship between experiences during the "anal crisis" (Neuman, 1973) and the genesis of racist behavior may be placed within a more inclusive developmental and sociocultural framework. Such an approach makes it possible to see how alienation in the cultural history of the West has also created conditions in the individual developmental situation for body devaluation—a phenomena arising from socialization experiences. It will be suggested that this development, a form of alienation from the body, having given rise to the possibilities for scapegoating in the Jew or the black man, creates additional psychosocial conditions sufficient for the development of further body devaluation in the victim.

Before proceeding to the developmental aspects of this situation, a digression, to place the whole question of the body image in its perspective, is presented. The possibility that an individual's body has an internal representation arose from the work of Pare, who reported his experiences with amputees during the sixteenth century (Kolb, 1959). Interest in the notion of the body image progressed slowly until the present century, when this interest gained momentum after Gerstmann's description of a case of finger agnosia in 1924 (Critchley, 1953). By the time Gerstmann described his syndrome, Freud had formulated his theory of erogenous zones of the body as well as their relationship with individual development. His theories were later elaborated upon by various revisionists mainly of the interpersonal, ego-object relations position represented in the body image literature by Schilder (1935, 1964) and Szasz (1957).

In general, concerns about the body and the body image remained for a considerable time in the medical disciplines of neurology and psychiatry. As early as 1935, Schilder suggested that the understanding of the psychological structure surrounding (representing) the body was one of the most important problems for psychology. But not until recently did psychologists respond to Schilder's concern by investigating that representation which he considered to be of such singular importance: Benton (1959); Witkin et al. (1962); Fisher & Cleveland (1968); Fisher (1970, 1973); Shontz (1969); and Gorman (1969).

This late entry of psychology into the area has meant, among other things, that the insights of developmental psychology have not benefited from a systematic introduction of body image constructs into the area. This limitation has led to the flourishing of a *reductionistic* developmental psychology, which has failed to take account of the development of body experience and awareness as part of the body-ego integration expressive of the biophysic unity of the growing individual. A good example of this reductionism is Allport (1955) who, in his now classical statement on "becoming" (personality and development) gives the body image construct a footnote status. But Allport is not alone in this limitation.

First, it should be emphasized that the reference here to the body and body image has little, if anything, to do with psychophysiology or even, for that matter, with the Freudian notion of id impulses. It is not a revisionist effort at refining psychonalytic instinct theory. The concern here is with the body image—its representation into a schema or gestalt, composed of various elements or schemata.

Psychodynamic theory, or what its devotees describe as "psychodynamic science," has made the most notable progress in attempting to explore the dynamic structure of the ego (Fairbairn, 1954; Guntrip, 1971). In one of the most lucid and systematic overviews of psychodynamic theory of "ego-object" relations theory, Guntrip summarizes developments in the following terms:

> I shall seek to show how the work of Melanie Klein became, in a subtle way (closely related to depth psychology), the unwitting originator of a similar major reorientation in the direction of object-relations theory from inside the psychoanalytic movement. From that time on, this stream of thought broadened irresistably. In distinction to the system-ego of Freud and Hartmann, a person-ego theory grew steadily in the work of W.R.D. Fairbairn and Erik Erikson, and is now coming to fruition in the work of Donald Winnicott and others in the child therapy field. The person-ego theory shows how the very beginnings of the ego growth as the core of self-hood in the psyche as a whole person is entirely bound up with the first and fundamental object relationship, that of the mother and her baby (p. 21).

In his review of the most important theoretical contributions on the development of ego-object relations and endopsychic structure, Guntrip explains that what has emerged from the contributions of a representative array of important theoreticians (Freud, Sullivan, Klein, Erikson, Hartmann, Winnicott, and Jacobson) is a recognition, following Fairbairn, that there is a three-fold pattern of ego splitting. The endopsychic structure is conceived of as consisting of a *libidinal ego,* an *anti-libidinal ego* and a *central ego,* to which Guntrip adds his own notion of the *schizoid regressed* or *withdrawn ego.* It is evident from Guntrip's analysis that he is more than delighted with the move from what he describes as Freudian psychobiology to ego-object relations. In discussing Erikson's theory of the basic modes of relating of the child and the relationship between the child and different body zones, Guntrip comes close to a recognition of the body as an important element in the constitution of the "person-ego" (Guntrip, 1971):

Here psychodynamics goes beyond Freudian psychobiology in which the body is the source of powerful id-drives that dictate to a weak and superficial ego. I regard this view of a human being as made of evolutionary layers, in which dangerous unmodified survivals of the primitive past trouble the present as quite unacceptable. In psychodynamic science the opposite view is being worked out. The body, accepted as the biological substate and foundation of the mental or personal life, has become part of a greater whole in such a way that the actual functioning of the body is determined in enormously complex ways by the personal life it sustains (p. 86).

But Guntrip, like many other workers who have made and are making contributions to the psychology of development, is only paying nominal tribute to the body in his characterization of the person-ego. In this later statement, the *trans-substantial ego* —the abstract disembodied ego of reductionist psychodynamics—emerges into obvious prominence. Guntrip (1971) writes:

Once we substitute for this speculative idea the concept of a psychosomatic whole with the ego-potential, developing primarily libidinally in object-relations, but also aggressively if thwarted, then the ego is the whole *psychic person, the psychic aspect of the basic psychosomatic whole being* (p. 135) [Italics added].

Guntrip has been quoted fairly extensively in order to suggest that there is, indeed, a serious theoretical issue to be addressed. But before formulating this issue, a look at another point of view by (Blatt & Ritzler, 1974). In this discussion of thought disorder and "boundary" disturbances in schizophrenia, they observe:

Disturbances in maintaining boundaries have also been noted in interpersonal relations in schizophrenia where there is an inordinate need and fear of merging and fusing in which both fusion and separateness result in experiences of an-

60

nihilation and dissolution. . . . Boundary disturbances in schizophrenia primarily involve difficulties maintaining a separation between independent objects (including self-nonself) and between internal experiences and external events (p. 3).

The concept of boundary has been used in what Blatt and Ritzler consider a different, more inclusive sense by Fisher and Cleveland (1968) and by Fisher (1962, 1963). When Fisher and Cleveland refer to a boundary in their discussions of the body image they mean the *body boundary*. Blatt and Ritzler appear to refer to an operationally defined boundary between self (ego) and nonself. Here is a theoretical issue which requires resolution. One construct refers to a body-ego constellation, the other to a self as opposed to the nonself. This difference dramatizes most clearly the dilemma of psychology and psychodynamics with respect to the body. A trans-substantial ego gives rise to an equally trans-substantial or abstract notion of boundary, a development which promises to result in a theoretical vicious circle. In spite of this difficulty, the theoretical and practical value of the boundary construct is beyond dispute. What should create concern is the fact that the theory relating to the development of this boundary during development is a problem that awaits study within the context of body representation.

Ego-object relations and representation theory both maintain that the ego is made up of several egos (Fairbairn, 1954). This multiplicity of egos arises from the interactions the child has with its mother during development. As the child develops its relations with its mother and other significant others, it also develops relations and representations of those objects. The body is, for the individual, in a dialectical sense both subject and object. During development, it too is the object of complex affects, relations and

61

adequate mental representation. Indeed, the reality of this representation has been sufficiently recognized (Schilder, 1935, 1964). Henry Head (Schilder, 1935) developed his view of the postural schema from the notion that, during development, the child develops representations (schemata) of body postures. The various schemata of the different postural positions of the body are gradually integrated into a total schema during the process of individuation. The knowledge of one's body which is developed into the self-constellation is not reflective knowledge but implicit knowledge. The postural representations of one's body are also integrated with schemata representing the visual and tactile-kinesthetic elements of the total gestalt of the body. This total representation constitutes the body image; an image which has to be integrated into the person-ego or self-system.

Whatever else one may prefer to believe, the reality of the representation of the body is no longer in question. In surgical practice, phantom limb states continue to validate the notion of body representation. Since this is so, we are compelled to recognize this reality and to include it actively in any attempt to theorize about development. The following section represents a beginning attempt to explore individuation on the basis of such an integrative approach.[2]

The study of the child's body-world falls within the general area of the psychodynamics of child development. The body is, for the child, part of its ever-expanding world. Body experience and representation are an integral part of the complex process of self-differentiation during development. To this extent, the study of the child's body-world must be seen and conceptualized within the context of general development but, more specifically, the development of the ego. The focus will be on the ways in which the child emerges from its primary unity with its mother (the primal relationship of Neumann, 1973) into a *polarized consciousness.* During the process of self-differentiation, the child's experience assumes the character of a polarization, not only one mediating the conscious and unconscious processes but also one differentiating subject (self-system or person-ego) from object(s) representing external reality. From a developmental point of view, these two polarizations are the main ones characteristic of the adult consciousness. They may, therefore, be described as the *primary polarizations.* In addition, the child must, in the process of individuation, achieve other polarizations related more to the postural elements of the body image (*secondary polarizations*). The representations of these polarizations assume the gradients of up-down, back-front and left-right.

It is Neumann's view that from conception to the end of the first post-uterine year, the growing child is literally in unity with its mother. This unitary reality has the character of a cosmic ("oceanic") experience of being, which the mother nourishes and confirms through her mothering through the establishment of that trust that is so important for the growing individual. The womb-like security characteristic of the mother-child matrix in non-pathological situations makes it possible during the earliest stages of development for the child's being (self) to be projected and expressed through its mother and her activities. For this reason one of the most important tasks in the child's ego development is the retrieval of its bodily self from the mother-self.

One of the more profound implications of the psychoanalytic theory of erogenous zones in child development is the focus it has directed to the fact that in more than a literal sense, the child's body is brought into prominence prior to the emergence of the ego. But before this birth of the bodily consciousness, before the body becomes the primary preoccupation of the developing child, the body is part of the undifferentiated mother-child constellation. Neumann (1973) describes this unity as follows:

> This unity on which the child's existence depends consists in a biopsychic identity between body and world, in which the child and mother, hungry body and appeasing breasts are one (pp. 11-12).

For purposes of the study of the child's body-world and how that body-world contributes to the child's overall development, it is preferrable to refer to the erogenous zones as *gnoseogenous* zones following Neumann. This means that the body areas of greatest sensitivity during development are existentially and psychologically more than erogenous in that they have a *relational* and cognitive character. This emphasis on the relational character of these zones has also been recognized and described by Erikson who identifies six basic modes of relating by the child (Guntrip, 1971).

Differentiation (individuation) in own body awareness, a development contingent on the status of the child's sensory modalities and general maturational status, progresses slowly and reaches its fullest development not only in a polarization in body representation but also in a unitary personal identity constellation. The progress and structure of the development of these representations, which lead to a polarization of the child's body experience, are amenable only to general treatment within the scope of the present study. Emphasis is deliberately placed on the development of body representation because the other elements of the development of ego-object relations and representation have received ample treatment in the psychodynamic literature.

As a general proposition, there are three basic orientations characteristic of the developing child. The first of these is the orientation towards *survival*. It is this orientation which Neumann (1973) describes as the "alimentary drive." It manifests itself throughout the body and is of the body. The second orientation is an *exploratory* one, while the third is a *possessive* one. Neumann's characterization of the unitary reality with its "participation mystique" has been adopted as the point of departure for the study of the development of the child's body-world. This position is adopted in full awareness that some workers of the ego-object relations position would consider such a view untenable; they would argue that the mother-child relationship is threatened with disruption as early as the first year of life because conflicts may develop around the oral sphere. But Neumann's formulation is preferred because it represents one of those rare instances in which the development of body awareness is taken into account in the explorations of self-differentiation from the mother-child relationship.

In the unitary reality, in the primal experience of the child's being one with its mother, the child is exposed to a variety of mothering experiences in nondistress situations. The child is bathed, kept warm and dry and fed almost on demand. This almost dictatorial posture of the child ensures and involves a great deal of physical contact between the child and its mother. This contact with the mother through the body surface (skin) is of paramount importance in development. At the appropriate stage of neuro-psychologic maturation, the body surface acquires significance as an experiential area mainly in two respects. First, the body surface mediates a representational function through the tactile and kinesthetic modalities, which contribute to the child's stream of bodily sensations. Second, these sensory experiences help the child in the development of the primary polarization of itself as subject against external objects. A bounding effect is achieved by these representations and polarizations through the body surface.

Emphasis should be placed on the fact that this bounding character of the child's body surface achieves significance particularly at that stage during development when the child is able to explore its own body surface with its hands and eyes. Bounding activity at this level may be described as *omnibus* in the sense that it involves the body as a whole.

The child's survival orientation is realized through sucking activity. This activity is not only essential for the child's well-being but concretely expresses the child's orientation towards the world. Here again, the relational quality of sucking, reinforced by associated gratifications, forms part of the bounding activity of the child through the oral region of the body. Progressively during development, food intake and little explorations of the body surface continue to give credence to the boundary-creating character of the oral region separating inside from outside. This experiential significance of the oral region of the body is rendered complete when the full circle of the "alimentary drive"—the intake of food through the mouth and its later evacuation through the anus as feces—is integrated into the child's experiential repertoire. In addition to the survival orientation of the child, the oral region shares with other zones of greater sensitivity the function of mediating the exploratory orientation of the child. Various objects and its own body parts, such as fingers and feet, become the subjects of this exploration.

The bounding activity of the oral region is supported during appropriate stages of development by the child's eyes and hands. Experientially, the three body organs (mouth, hands, eyes) identified so far share the attribute of incorporation (grasping) which is so fundamental to cognitive activity. They are relational organs capable at

66

critical stages of development of mediating distance, relations and, ultimately, bounding activity. The scanning activity involved in the exploratory orientation of the child is effected through the mouth and hands which explore the child's own body surface, that of its mother and the surface and form of external objects. This activity is supported by accompanying visual exploration of the reality and form of the child's own body, the bodies of others and external reality. The intricate processes involved in this activity have been dealt with by Schilder (1935) and by Merleau-Ponty (1964), in his discussion of the "mirror image."

The exploratory and survival orientations of the child form various permutations at different stages of development. Related to these orientations is the "possessive" orientation characterized by Brown (1966) as follows:

> The possessive orientation originates in what Freud calls instinctual ambivalence, i.e., the split between "good" and "bad," love and hatred, Eros and Thanatos. The aim of the possessive orientation is to keep the loved object entire and intact: to separate and keep the good, to separate and expel the bad (p. 145).

This possessive orientation of the child is one of the radical (root) dynamics in the process of splitting both of the child's personality and its experience and representation of its body.

The discussion thus far suggests that the process of self-differentiation—the child's retrieval and withdrawal from its unity with its mother—has its primary origins in the three orientations of the developing child. These orientations during the earliest stages of development anticipate the *transactional* (relational) character of the adult consciousness. The initial experience of the body is diffuse and primitive; despite the progressive development of the primary polarization between subject and object, the child's body experience is still relatively free from the secondary polarizations of the postural schema.

With increased neuromuscular control, conditions are created for the development of the secondary representations and polarizations. The exploratory orientation of the child, which progressively receives impetus from the maturation of the child, literally enables it to bump itself against the world. As soon as the child achieves the developmental milestones of being able to sit, crawl and walk, it increases its chances of experiencing disruptive pain or discomfort originating from its surroundings. The significance of pain or discomfort inflicted from outside is the disruptive effect it has on the child's experience of unity with its mother and its world. This disruption, except in cases where it may have dramatic results, is meaningful to the child to the extent it helps the child develop a space equilibrium around itself (personal space)—a bounding activity of radical importance in the development of both a polarized consciousness and the representation of the postural schema.

Motility and the adoption of postural positions are milestones in the general development of the child and in the development of body representation. The adoption of the erect posture, the child's ability to move about as well as its improving capacity for symbolization opens up the adult world and makes it possible for the child to be open and sensitive to experiences relating to its own body. Up to the point of the adoption of the erect posture, the child has been involved in various body boundary defining activities relating to its body as a whole. The development of the postural model of the body is achieved through a polarization in the child's consciousness—a polarization in the interest of boundary definition and self-differentiation. It is now appropriate to make some observations regarding the secondary representations and polarization subserving the postural schema.

The demarcation of personal space and the creation of a space equilibrium necessary for navigation demands that the gradients up-down, back-front, left-right progressively be experienced and integrated by the growing child as part of its survival and relational orientation. But the development of these gradients should be seen as aiding the child in the process of integrating the representation of its emerging body image. Were it not for a particular kind of socialization, the mastering of directionality with regard to the various gradients would, in all probability, be of equal significance. Among the different gradients of the body, the up-down polarization has suffered most from sociocultural overvaluation and devaluation. The symbolism of this sociocultural valuation consists of the value-loaded oppositions between light and dark, good and evil, heaven and earth, soul and body, cleanliness and dirt, God and devil (Neumann, 1973). In a previous section of this study the devaluation and subsequent alienation from the body was shown to develop from an elaborate system of symbols in opposition. The origins of these symbolic oppositions, arose from a dualistic ethic and a repressive civilization.

Parents have been making this variety of symbols available to growing children in modern industrialized societies. In the act of mothering and socializing the child, through which complex sociocultural processes have become ritualized, these symbolic oppositions are subtly transmitted to the growing child. At that stage when the child is able to walk (the adoption of the erect posture), toilet training is also introduced as one of the child's developmental tasks. The psychological difficulties that arise in some, if not most, cases with regard to the socialization of children vis-à-vis the body usually are not reflective of disturbed functioning in an individual family. Although, in general, it is reasonable to assume that unique elements will be involved in any situation, it is more likely that the cultural canon will take precedence over individual predisposition.

As long as societies continue in their devaluation of the body, mothers are unlikely to have healthy attitudes toward their own bodies, least of all towards those of their developing children. But not only body devaluation creates problems regarding the body for today's mothers; they also suffer because of cultural standardization of the female body. Fisher (1973) has described this process:

> Body depersonalization is actually encouraged by many of our current customs and fads. The woman who is repeatedly confronted by clothing style changes that she is supposed to adopt, whether or not they are compatible to her own feelings about her body, comes to perceive her body as not terribly different from a department store mannequin. Her body is simply one more standardized frame and, as such, seems perhaps to belong more to the culture than to herself. The force of this body standardization is highlighted if you consider that it applies not only to a woman's outer clothing, but also her underwear, her hair style, the cosmetics she applies to her face, fingers, and toes, the respectable limits of the kind of aroma she can emit, and even the angle or tilt of her breasts (p. 14).

Referring specifically to socialization, Fisher points out:

> The truth is that our culture is dedicated to blunting the individual's skill in interpreting body experiences. Most "advanced" cultures strive for rationality and regard body arousal as likely only to mislead or to introduce irrationality into decision making. The child is taught to make decisions "with his head." If he says he does not "feel like" doing something this is usually regarded as a pretty flimsy basis for action. Action must be based on rational "reasons" rather

than body feelings. Even basic body feelings like hunger or the need to defecate are typically relegated to the control of more cognitively oriented schedules, which dictate when it is proper to respond to such feelings (pp. 10-11).

Prior to the toilet training stage, the child's ego is still relatively uncontaminated by the cultural standards relating to cleanliness. He places no valuation on his feces which are experienced as part of his body configuration. Active intervention by the mother during the second year of life demands that the child achieve, as quickly as possible, a body-ego integration exclusive of excrement and its associated feelings. The body-ego integration required in accordance with the societal standards of bodily cleanliness is one involving, at least in the fantasy of the child, a clean, pure and almost ethereal body dominated by rationality. The alienation from the body that accompanies the sociocultural devaluation of the lower pole of the body is compensated for by an overvaluation of the upper pole, experienced as the seat of the ego and spirituality (Neumann, 1973).[3] The parallel between this polarization of the body and that between heaven (spirituality, good, purity) and earth (sin, evil, dirt) is complex in its historical development but is evident. Here it will suffice merely to point out that, since a literal amputation of the devalued part of the body for purposes of achieving the culturally desired body-ego integration is impossible, the child achieves an "anal castration" in fantasy (Neumann, 1973). Later discussion will focus on the significance of the polarization in body representation and its dynamic relationship with the ontogenesis of racist behavior.

At this point, two key concepts should be identified and dealt with in terms of child development: body image and sociological schema. Both constructs refer to body representation. First, what is generally described as the

71

body image, a concept which embraces the subsidiary visual and postural representations (Schemata) of the body, must be considered the earlier development in body relations and representation. It is a representation of the body which, like other representations of external objects, is developed through an integration of sensory data and symbolic forms (language) available in a particular culture. Early differentiation and representation, through primary (boundary defining) and secondary polarizations, forms the somatic and existential basis for the development of the ego as personal identity. During the early differentiation from the mother-child matrix and later, a foundation is created for the representation of the body schema in the parietal cortex.

The individual schema or representation is idomatic and unique and is integrated with an individual's total self-system or ego. In spite of its nature, the body image as part of the ego constellation is not free from the effects of cultural standards. For this reason it is theoretically preferrable to talk in terms of the perceptual (postural schema) which is more bodily based in its cortical representation. However, a useful distinction between the postural schema and the body image is difficult to maintain in practice. This issue can be resolved in the following way.

In a theoretical formulation of the development of the child's emergence of its body representation, it is useful to introduce an additional construct to account for the dimension of the child's body. Such a concept is necessary to recognize that cultural standards of desirable and undesirable attributes are available. The concept that should be introduced is the notion of sociological schema of the body used in another context by Kouwer (1953). As was seen earlier, this construct is even more useful in accounting for certain varieties of alienation from the body, particularly in race supremacist cultures. Within the context of individual development, it is necessary to posit this concept over and above that of the individual schema. The extreme example of the sociological schema is the body stereotype, either expressive of an *overvaluation* or *undervaluation* of the body. Under certain conditions, such as the situations of the black man and the Jew discussed earlier, the individual and sociological representations of the body may be set in opposition. The ideal is for these schemata of the body to be sufficiently integrated into the person-ego.

This discussion of the development of the child's body-world provides a necessary theoretical framework for the analysis of racism as a form of scapegoating related to alienation from the body during socialization. In racist environments, where sociological schemata of the body are developed with abandon, the body-ego integration is always threatened with disruption. In addition, a desirable integration between the individual and sociological schema becomes difficult to achieve and leads to splitting processes that remind one of ego splitting. In the development of body representation, two factors stand out as deserving special consideration in this disruption. The first is the *anal crisis* which arises from the cultural devaluation of the body's lower pole.[4] The second factor is the availability in race supremacist societies, of clearly developed sociological schemata of the body to be used as targets for scapegoating purposes. The disruption of the body-ego integration leads to the alienation from one's body as one of its more dramatic consequences—a result of socialization experiences supported by one's experience in the wider sociocultural context.

The consequences of the polarization in body representation into an upper (head) pole and lower (anal and vital) pole are stated explicitly by Neumann (1973):

> The ego, which is dependent on guidance by the Self, cuts itself off in opposition to the Self, which as totality-Self and

73

body-Self encompasses also the rejected lower aspect of the body and world, and, by introjecting the negatively evaluating group conscience, bases itself on the super-ego representing the cultural canon. The means by which it thus cuts itself off from and opposes itself to the Self—and thereby to its own nature—are the same as those employed by the group for this purpose—compulsion, suppression and repression. This split of the personality gives rise to aggressions which either are projected outward in a destructive, moralistic effort to destroy evil in others (scapegoat psychology) or else—when this is not entirely successful—lead to an intensification of the guilt feelings which continue to nourish the circular process of taboo and self-defense (p. 133).

The imposition during socialization of anal cleanliness through rigorous methods of toilet training and devaluation of the lower pole creates a crisis for some growing children. The threat to the child's sense of well-being arises from the fantasy of anal castration in which the child's sense of completeness in body experience is impaired. This impairment is not limited to body experience because it also results in negative self-evaluation which creates conflict within the ego (self-system) catastrophically resolved through a splitting of the personality. This split takes the general form characteristic of all of the child's relations with objects, namely a distinction between a "good" me which is cherished and a "bad" me which is the victim of the most violent denial and rejection. It is important to emphasize that the split in endopsychic structure which accompanies the anal crisis is the most critical one with respect to body representation. Other splits arise because of ego-object relations and representations at various other levels, such as the interpersonal sphere of interaction.

In general, therefore, the socialization constellation carries with it a lethal potential for the developing ego, not only with repsect to body representation but also in relation to other ego-object relationships. The particular dif-

74

ficulties of this time give the four-tier ego, consisting of a central ego, libidinal ego, anti-libidinal ego and a schizoid regressed ego. Negative self-evaluation associated with impaired body representation leads to a split from awareness of this portion of the body schema. This part of the schema with its associated affects goes to the unconscious with other bad objects only to return with tensions that compel individuals and groups to find targets (scapegoats). Even in the history of industrial society, the process of psychic splitting has been identified consistently as the major source of alienation and mass phenomena such as racism. The child's view of the world in the present cultural climate of the West is determined in important respects during the anal crisis. During one of the emotion-loaded periods, the dualistic conception of the world into good and bad is concretely dramatized.

Earlier the alienation of modern man was referred to and an important dimension of this problem was identified as being man's alienation from the reality of his body. Following Neumann (1973), the culturally available symbolism that sustains the polarization of the body representation into an upper and lower pole was described. This interpretation is consistent with the most general hypothesis concerning the origins of racist behavior and attitudes during development. It can be described as a hypothesis of the blackness-dirt and/or blackness-evil equation. Cardinal to the formulation of this hypothesis are the positions accorded to the symbolism of the anal crisis and the psychological mechanisms of projection and introjection. The projection hypothesis has been used by a number of investigators to account for the dynamics of black-white interaction (Cytrynbaum, 1972).

Some studies have shown that at an early developmental stage white children develop the equation between blackness and dirt/feces (Goodman, 1964; McDonald,

1970). The most inclusive and categorical of the available equations are those between whiteness and *mind* as opposed to blackness and body. Cleaver (1968) identified these equations as constituting the categories of "Omnipotent Administrator" (white male); "Ultrafeminine" (white female); "Supermasculine Menial" (black male) and "Black Amazon" (black female). These sterotypes or sociological schemata basically reflect a single dichotomy between mind and body, expressive of Western man's alienation from his body—the polarization between up and down, good and evil. This basic polarization, through various unconscious elaborations, created the unconscious (irrational) social structuring for black-white interaction throughout history.

For white children, the difficulties arising from the development of a negative self-evaluation are cushioned in racist environments by a negative sociological schema of the black body that has developed over time. Like the body of the Jew, the black body was tagged with all the anti-values of the Caucasian body. In the colonial and following situations of black-white interaction, the black body has become the repository of and target for all the bad objects in the collective psyche of the West—the stereotype for everything from dirt to evil. The sociological schema of the victim of racism has been made available for the adaptive resolution of the alienation of the racist from his own body.

But before giving brief illustrations of some of the difficulties black children have to contend with, brief references will be made to one example from the author's own experience.[5] There is one thing that is still very distinct in my memory of my early youth. This critical memorable event involves a man who was a respected member of our completely rural village. Like most able-bodied black men he used to return to his village at Christmas; about the only time when black migratory workers are able to spend time with their families. He was, by the standards of that situa-

76

tion, a very remarkable man indeed. Rumor had it that he spent about an hour doing his long hair, perhaps another thirty minutes cleaning his shoes and so on. He used to be the best dressed man in the village. We might even say, he was a one-eyed king in the kingdom of the blind. But together with these elements of his character was a well-known statement that he used to tag on everything he said with emphasis or indignation. He would, say: "*Ni Mulungu mina, ni base ndzeni*" meaning, "I am a white person, I am clean (white) inside." We say that this was remarkable because this statement left a very strong impression on all of us who had never seen a white man in our lives. In that village, the next white man was hundreds of miles away. The child growing up in a racist society bumps against these sociological representations at a time when even the body image is still not fully integrated.

Documented examples are given last in order to finish with the world of everyday experience. Again in South Africa, where apartheid is flourishing, a black child expressed at four years of age a disconcerting distrust of her dark skin. She would compare herself with other light-skinned children and verbalize what she experienced as her lack of beauty.

Self-perception in the experience of black children in the United States has been documented by several investigators (Deusch et al., 1968). Robert Coles (1970) discusses material concerning a black child named Ruby. Ruby was, for a considerable time, unable to use black and brown colors in her drawings of human and other figures. In addition, she drew "white people larger and more life-like;" she presented blacks as smaller and usually with body parts missing.

Coles' experience with Ruby is not a unique instance. A similar kind of ideation was evident with a group of albino children studied in Johannesburg, South Africa

(Manganyi, Kromberg, & Jenkins, 1974). In this group, negative self-evaluation emerged most clearly in the albino's rendering of the self-portrait as part of the draw-a-person-test. When the human figure drawings were analyzed using the Sophistication of Body Concept Scale (Witkin et al., 1962), it was found that the self-portrait drawings as a group revealed the most statistically significant number of primitive features.

Brief as these examples are, they are sufficient as indicators of the body representation problems of black children in racist societies. It is necessary to emphasize that socialization as a psychosocial process is not standard in all families in any one culture. For this reason, the relationships suggested in this analysis must be understood as qualified to the extent that there are an infinite number of possible variations both in terms of individual socialization and reactions to such socialization.

In racist societies, the resolution of the anal crisis in the case of black children is made difficult by the existence of the negative sociological schema of the black body espoused by such cultures and shared by black parents. Fanon (1967) who recognized the difficulties black people had in the development of body representation, presented the negative sociological schema in the following terms:

> My body was given back to me sprawled out, distored, recolored, clad in mourning in that white winter day. The Negro is an animal, the Negro is bad, the Negro is mean, the Negro is ugly; look, a nigger, it's cold, the nigger is shivering, the nigger is shivering because he is cold, the little boy is trembling because he is afraid of the nigger, the nigger is shivering with cold, that cold that goes through your bones, the handsome little boy is trembling because he thinks that the nigger is quivering with rage, the little white boy throws himself into his mother's arms: Mama, the nigger's going to eat me (pp. 113-14).

While the adaptive resolution of the split which arises from the polarization in body representation in the case of white children would appear to involve merely the dimensions of a "good" and "bad" pole, the black child must contend with a body that is stereotypically devalued as a totality. The severity of the problem for each child would appear to be associated with the degree to which his/her features deviate from the appeal characteristics of the white sociological schema. Children who are socialized to believe that their bodies are deviant from the desired attributes become victims of a process of negative self and group evaluation (experiencing their bodies as "bad objects"). This collusion between black parents and the race supremacist culture creates conditions favorable to the introjection of the attributes of the white sociological schema. Here it should be emphasized that the split between "good" and "bad" objects is not limited to the resolution of the difficulties arising from the anal crisis. Splitting is characteristic of the development of object relations and their representation in general. Emphasis on the anal crisis arises in part from a recognition of the part it plays in the development of the devaluation of the lower pole of the body.

In racist societies, the development of body representation is beset with difficulties for both black and white children. The general difficulties which influence the course of the socialization of children reflect industrial society's alienation from the body. The development of the sociological schemata of the "good" and "bad" bodies developed within the general context of alienated man as collective adaptive mechanisms for coping with both individual and collective psychological splitting accompanied the polarization of body representation into an upper and lower poles.

While the alienation from the body was expressing itself through the puritanical ladies who presented to Freud and Breuer during the last century, it had been and was being resolved on a large scale in Africa and elsewhere as part of the colonial black-white interaction. In the colonial situation, the different body of the African indigenous peoples provided a splendid medium for the scapegoat—for the projection of the alienated, devalued, polarized white body of the colonizer. As matters are today, that initial individual and collective solution is still ravaging the socialization of children in race supremacist societies.

NOTES

1. In *The Mass Psychology of Fascism*, (1970) Reich has clearly formulated the limitations of socioeconomic analysis of mass movements. Analysis, while taking sufficient account of economics and culture, must also be addressed toward man's "character structure"—the irrational substratum of man's conduct.

2. The general framework of the discussion on development is based primarily on Neumann (1973). The emphasis and main formulation of body related issues is the author's, except where indicated. Neumann does not focus primarily on body representation in his theory of child development. He remains, however, an outstanding example of the kind of integration in theory which is championed here, namely an approach towards child development which emphasizes and recognizes the emergence of body representation as an integral part of the ego constellation. His discussion of the development of the "bodily self" and the concept of "polarization" has been most fruitful in beginning to formulate a developmental framework for the study of body representation.

3. This cultural inflation of the ego-sphere is also recognized and emphasized by Reich (1970).

4. The devaluation of the lower pole of the body has not only been related to its association with excreta but also with taboos around sexuality (including masturbation) and menstruation. Although emphasis here is placed on "anality," it should always be remembered that the lower pole has a symbolic matrix encompassing all these bodily realities.

5. The author's own experience around body representation contamination was expressed in the following sketch written about a year ago:

it's always
always tinkering at something
invades my sinews and all

into the recesses of my being
a shadow
surrounds
mistifies my black being
is fused with it
that shadow
emissary of civilization
non-part of the cord which nourished me
nor the screamgasp
my throwness into the world
now as I sit here
there is a glowing darkness . . . .

CHAPTER IV

The "Body-for-Others"

Psychic splitting in the individual and collective levels has been identified in very different contexts as the most pronounced characteristic of man in modern society.[1] We have been concerned with this condition particularly with regard to its relationship and consequences for body experience. It could well be said that what has been discussed so far is "normal alienation from experience" (Laing, 1967). It turns out, in fact, that once habitual modes of thinking are abandoned, normality becomes a statistical issue which tells very little about the character of psychosocial reality.

The splits attendant upon "normal alienation" from experience are only qualitatively different from those which accompany schizoid phenomena in Laing's (1959) "divided self." What is being suggested here is that the schizoid condition represents a far more profound and dramatic manifestation of a form of alienation which is specific to modern industrial culture. What is normal alienation? Laing (1967) provides a characterization of this condition which is consistent, in important respects, with the point of view adopted in this study:

As adults, we have forgotten most of our childhood, not only its contents but its flavor; as men of the world, we hardly know of the existence of the inner world: we barely remember our dreams, and make little sense of them when we do; *as for our bodies, we retain just sufficient propriocep-tive sensations to coordinate our movements and to ensure the minimal requirements for biosocial survival—to register fatigue, signals for food, sex, defecation, sleep; beyond that, little or nothing . . . .*
What we call "normal" is a product of repression, denial, splitting, projection, introjection and other forms of destruc-tive action on experience. . . . It is radically estranged from the structure of being. . . . There are forms of alienation that are relatively strange to statistically "normal" forms of alienation. The normally alienated person, by reason of the fact that he acts more or less like everyone else, is taken to be sane (pp. 26, 27; italics added).

The "strange" forms of alienation which Laing is referr-ing to are the "schizoid condition" and schizophrenia dis-cussed more fully in his *The Divided Self* (1959). Most helpful for the present analysis in his formulation of the schizoid problem is his characterization of the "embodied" and "disembodied" selves. It may be useful, however, to refer briefly to some more general ideas before focusing specific attention around issues involving body experience. Laing distinguishes two existential conditions: ontological security and insecurity. Under conditions of ontological security:

The individual . . . may experience his own being as real, alive, whole; as differentiated from the rest of the world in ordinary circumstances so clearly that his identity and autonomy are never in question; as a continuum in time; as having an inner consistency, substantiality, genuineness, and worth; as spatially coextensive with the body (p. 41).

Where ontological security is absent:

> The individual in the ordinary circumstances of living may feel more unreal than real; in a literal sense, more dead than alive; precariously differentiated from the rest of the world, so that his identity and autonomy are always in question. He may lack the experience of his own temporal continuity. He may not possess an over-riding sense of personal consistency or cohesiveness. He may feel more insubstantial than substantial, and unable to assume that the stuff he is made of is genuine, good, valuable. And he may feel his self as partially divorced from his body (p. 42).

Under conditions of normal alienation, conditions of splitting, repression, and denial and scapegoating, the split between the *body* and *mind* becomes possible and real. The disembodied schizoid individual is not alone or unique in his marked tendency to experience his being as polarized between body and psyche. He only becomes more adept than his brethren in the culture. Something can be learned, however, from his condition—his relationship with his body. As a result of the radical nature of his alienation from his body, he presents an unusual opportunity (a magnified portrait) for the study of phenomena that are more concealed in the conditions of "normal alienation."

Ontological security, or what is termed here "authentic being," may be described as an existential status in which the body exists for-me and through-me before it becomes the body-for-others. Laing (1959) has offered the following useful formulation to express this reality: ([self/body] = other). In the alienated state, in the conditions of incompleteness which characterize the situations of the racist and the victim of racism, the body becomes and is experienced predominantly as the body-for-others (self = [body/other]).

It may be necessary here to re-emphasize that being authentic is a kind of *situatedness* in one's body, with others, objects, space and time. The nexus of this situatedness is the core reality represented in being embodied in a body which constitutes a point of reference and departure for all the fundamental relations with the other. The case of Peter, reported and discussed in some detail by Laing (1959) is a dramatic instance, not only of internal psychic splitting between body and self (ego) but also of what is termed "trans-substantial ego."

> Peter was a large man of twenty-five, and he looked the picture of health. He came to see me complaining that there was a constant unpleasant smell coming from him. He could smell it clearly, but he was not sure whether it was the sort of smell that others could smell. He thought that it came particularly from the lower part of his body and the genital region. In the fresh air, it was like the smell of burning, but usually it was a smell of something sour, rancid, old, decayed. He likened it to the sooty, gritty, musty smell of a railway waiting-room; or the smell that comes from the broken-down "closets" of the slum tenements of the district in which he grew up. He could not get away from this smell although he had taken to having several baths a day (p. 120).

In addition to Peter's presenting problem, Laing gives other pertinent details. Some notable features in Peter's situation are that he was an only child who was not spoiled during his childhood; instead, his parents were, to say the least, markedly indifferent to his presence and growing needs.

For two parents who were self-absorbed, Peter was an unwelcome intruder. Peter's mother was vanity personified. Not only did she treasure any clothes her husband could buy her, but she had anxieties around the possibilities of being disfigured through childbirth. She was committed to a false bodily vitality—the "body-for-others"—the sociological schema.[2] Her husband was no different because he not only succeeded in nourishing her vanity but basked in it. That was not all. Peter's mother

86

threw her superstitions about the body at him, when she caught him playing with his penis, by saying "that it wouldn't grow if he did that." Her husband was even more represenative of the cultural prudishiness. In belittling Peter, he would call him "Useless Eustace" and go on to say that he was "just a big lump of dough."

A penis that would not grow and a lump of dough are expressions which could hardly portend well for the bodily well-being of a growing boy. In his discussion of the material, Laing begins by pointing out that Peter had not been offered the developmental opportunity of feeling and being "at home" both in his body and in the world. When he presented to Laing at twenty-five years of age, he had reached a point in his development at which he experienced his body as unreal and literally dead.

> His preoccupation with being seen, I believe, an attempt to recoup himself from his underlying feeling that he was nobody (had no body). There was a primary inadequacy in the reality of his own experience of himself as embodied and it was out of this that his preoccupation with his body-for-others arose, i.e. his body as seeable, hearable, smellable, touchable by the other. No matter how painful this "self"-consciousness was to him, it arose inevitably out of the fact that his own body experiences were so uncoupled from his self that he needed the awareness of himself as a real object to assure himself, by his roundabout route, that he had a tangible existence (p. 127).

This is an instance of a self (ego) which has become in-substantial or trans-substantial. Laing makes some additional observations relating to Peter's experience of his body. Peter had fantasies about "anal intercourse" and the "production of children made of feces." He was convinced that the substantiality of his body consisted of something rotten and worthless. What Laing emphasizes in his discussion of Peter's problems, is the fact that Peter tried desperately, through the development of his presenting problem to keep his experience of the reality of his body alive.

The split between the body and the self which is sometimes observed in the schizoid condition is not unique to this condition. It represents a magnification of a split which is actively promoted by advanced cultures in their socialization of children. Part of Peter's socialization amounted to conditions which led to profound negative self-evaluation: His father characterized him as "just a lump of dough" (shit?)—useless! Mother told him his penis was going to be stunted.

Within Peter's socialization, the messages relating to the body were loud and clear. On the one hand, there was mother's body which had to be protected from being disfigured. It had to remain attractive and sexy. Peter's mother represented an instance of the culturally idealized sociological schema of the body. Since the sociological schema is statistical, normative and not vital or idiomatic (uniquely individual), it is an epiphenomenon. The body as sociological schema is developed and experienced as an object for the other's perception— touch, smell and visual appreciation. Peter's mother was herself alienated from the vital reality of her own body and her anxiety around her body assumed various subtle and obvious forms: identifying childbirth with disfigurement and fantasies of castration generated around Peter's play with his penis.

His father added to his wife's devaluation of the lower pole of Peter's body by adding to the fantasies about castration, the equation of feces with worthlessness. Peter had fantasies about anal intercourse and children made out of feces. It is not surprising that the smell that led Peter to seek a consultation emanated from the devalued lower part of his body.

In Peter's socialization constellation, modern society's alienation from the body is presented in microcosm. In it are represented the deceptive and alienating (dehumanizing) *vital values* of the sociological schema of the body (self = [body/other]). The values of cleanliness, sex appeal and so on were highly regarded. These vital values are curiously enough only brought into prominence by the concurrent existence, as in the culture in general, of anti-values (smell, for example) subserving the polarization of the body into an upper and lower pole. Both the vital values and anti-values support society's socialization of the body-for-others (self = [body/other]) as opposed to the existentially given body-for-me/through-me ([self/body] = other).

In advanced cultures, the body-for-others has become the societal norm as suggested by Fisher's (1973) notion of the female body as one that has become a "standardized frame." It may well be true that, since modern cultures in the West thrive on the devaluation and standardization of the body, people such as Peter with his split between self and body dramatize, for the culture, a reality which is too disconcerting to deal with, namely that splitting processes are at the very core of individual and collective consciousness. The schizoid individual is certainly not alone in his alienation and trans-substantiality. The racist and his victim have elaborated the culturally available alienation from the body. In the course of time, the racist developed a body aesthetic and postive sociological schema to compensate for the discomfort he experienced from his alienation from his body. Since he experienced the existential giveness of his body as consisting also of anti-values, (smell, genitality, etc.), it is not surprising that he was later to project these anti-values on to his victims and to develop negative sociological schemata consistent with anti-values. The victim of racism, lost his authenticity by allowing himself to be caught between a desire to reject the given reality of his body and the incorporation of the attributes of the white sociological schema. Both these aims are, in the nature of the situation, unattainable. It turns out in fact that the idealized sociological schema and its vital values is an illusory package for both the racist and his victim. What appears to be required in both situations is the elimination of all the unrealistic sociological schemata of the body—a cultural movement away from the body-for-others to the body-for-me/through-me—a return to authentic being.

It would not have been necessary to point out that psychology and related disciplines should lead the way in the progressive elimination of the divided self in modern societies, if psychology had not been indifferent to the sociocultural development of the trans-substantial self. Psychology has yet to address itself to the *person* as a whole. We have argued that the development of the individual includes the development of body representation as one of the most important elements in the socialization constellation.

Frankl is convinced that "existential frustration" and the futility and personal dislocation from experience (noegenic neuroses) arise from man's failure to confront and actualize meaning. It is a spiritual sterility, an all-encompassing emptiness ("existential vacuum") which engulfs the men and women who despair to the office of the psychotherapist or logotherapist. True enough, Frankl is acutely aware of the social reality which encourages the development of a world-view which eschews the sphere of meaning and values. His discussion of this reality, however, fails to provide a convincing account of the psychosocial substratum; the breeding ground of the condition of alienation. This is another way of saying that the sociocultural factors singled out by Frankl are relevant but inadequate in their explanatory value. A search for more convincing accounts leads not only to the recognition of the leveling quality of modern conformist cultures but to the even more important area of socialization.

Having discussed socialization within the context of the development of body representation and the schizoid condition, some of the additional conditions responsible for the condition of existential inauthenticity can be examined. The problem of meaning and values will be disregarded, for a moment, in order to direct attention on the infant-mother constellation, to identify some of the ways in which it has come to be abused by society as well as its general contribution to the condition of alienation.

The special position of the family in the study of society arises not only from its socialization function but also from the fact that the family is the most reliable index of the general condition of the total society of which it is a part. Uncertainty in the area of values in society as a whole is reflected in an equally evident and predictable confusion in the family. To give an example, it may be expected that society's current uncertainty about the status of women in society in general should be reflected as a kind of endemic role confusion within families, along with all the associated problems which may reasonably be expected to accompany such confusion. Society and its psychologists after Freud's monumental discoveries, appears to have succeeded in inducing guilt in growing numbers of mother. This effect has been achieved in various ways.

Freud drew attention to the significance, for the developing self (personality) of the first five years of life. The significance of socialization experiences during this period was, following Freud's discoveries, researched and documented (Van den Berg, 1972). Important insights on the mother-child relationship were formulated as a result of increased interest in problems related to what came to be known as *maternal deprivation*. A message and, more aptly,

91

a "commandment" emerged that was directed at mothers: love thy child as thy self. Commandments by their very nature are categorical and tend to generate guilt both in their devotees and non-conformists. The idea of a mother's love of her child became problematic because the whole notion of love is something which is itself unclear in Western culture as a whole (van den Berg, 1972).

Even more important, the insights that developed around the mother-child relationship became ritualized into behavioral prescriptions for mothers, in kind, to prescriptions for a balanced diet. The unique, distinctive and profoundly idiomatic character of each mother-child interaction was disregarded in the enthusiasm that followed the discoveries of the significance of early socialization. Equally significant is the fact that judgment could be passed, on individual mothers by society and even more often by mothers themselves, on failures of socialization. But it turns out, on closer scrutiny that most often, where such failures have occured, they can usually be found to have resulted from combined individual and societal pressures.

It is common-place to say that present-day mothers have become victims of an erratic barrage of contradictory yet powerful pressures for standardization of socialization practices. These contradictory messages have come from the mental health professions and the popular press. Yet lonely, unheard voices have been raised against this interference between the mother and her child. Winnicott (1957), who may be recognized as one of the foremost thinkers in this area, has observed:

> Administrative tidiness, the dictates of hygiene, a laudable urge toward the promotion of bodily health, these and all sorts of other things get between the mother and her baby, and it is unlikely that mothers themselves will rise up in concerted effort to protest against interference . . . .

92

We all join forces in enabling the emotional relationship between the mother and her new baby to start and to develop naturally (pp. 201, 203).

Winnicott's profound, two-fold concern, which he shares with Neumann, is about the character of the mother-child relationship and its implication for the development of the self; and, more important within the present context, the significance of motherhood for society as a whole.

To begin with the first concern, Winnicott is not didactic or prescribing because he mainly suggests that there are ideal and natural conditions which may be found in the mother-child relationship. These are the conditions of the "good enough environment" in which the level of self-consciousness in the mother's behavior towards her infant is most minimal. In the conditions of "primary maternal preoccupation" (the "participation mystique" of Neumann), the mother is more uniquely herself and yet expressive of something transpersonal or general to *homo sapiens*. The special and heightened sensitivity of the mother is nurturing to the child's developing self; while mothers "who do therapy," instead of being good mothers, introduce conditions which are lethal to the child's developing ego (Winnicott, 1958):

> On the other hand, without the initial good-enough environmental provision, this self that can afford to die never develops. The feeling of real is absent and if there is not too much chaos the ultimate feeling is of futility. The inherent difficulties in life cannot be reached, let alone the satisfactions. If there is not chaos, there appears a false self that hides the true self, that complies with demands, that reacts to stimuli, that rids itself of instinctual experiences by having them, but that is only playing for time (pp. 304-5).

Feelings of unreality, futility and the development of a defensive primitive "false self" would probably be recognized by Fairbairn, Guntrip and certainly Laing as characteristic of the schizoid condition. Guilt-ridden, anxious mothers are products of modern culture (van den Berg, 1972) and it is reasonable to expect that most of them become socioculturally programmed to "do therapy" with children rather than provide those conditions which are natural to the mother-child relationship. If this trend is as significant and wide-spread as Winnicott and van den Berg suggest, the social implications for alienation must continue to be of radical importance. One issue is decided. The "divided" and incomplete self is a mode of being-in-the-world fostered by culture and its socialization dimension. Seen in this light, alienation becomes an environmental (socialization) deficiency condition in the same sense as the psychoses are sometimes described as environmental deficiency diseases.

But to see the problem as others have, as one primarily involving pathological limitations on the part of mothers, is to beg the question. In the most ideal sociocultural conditions, the mother's contribution to society, to its relative freedom from alienation, would be something so self-evident as to require no emphasis. This emphasis has become more than necessary since society has not only succeeded in vitiating the mother's natural disposition for good-enough mothering but has also added and aroused guilt in most mothers.

The emphasis in the child development literature and the popular press has been on the disruptive potential of mothers with respect to the healthy development of children. The reality of this position may be brought out most clearly with an example from pediatric practice in a racist environment. Communities are known for their neglect of the needs and problems of the poor—usually the victims of racism. It is not uncommon in such circumstances for families to be so poor as to be unable to afford the bare necessities of life. Children in such populations suffer from nutritional deficiency diseases. What happens when such a child is ill and taken to a pediatrician tells something about the desensitizing effects of privilege. The doctor may look at the child and chide the mother in lofty tones for not giving the child a chance in the world. What gets lost in the doctor's enthusiasm is a self-evident reality, namely that society and not the mother is the main offender. Society fails to provide the child's mother with a reasonable chance, and it is indeed profound arrogance to suggest that this kind of mother could give anybody a chance in her situation of distress.

What is true about nutrition is true with regard to the psychological well-being of the developing child. Here again, mothers carry the blame for almost anything which may go astray in the developmental situation. It is they who deprive. Nobody would deny that some mothers fail to be creative, natural and sensitive for individual reasons. But to stop at this recognition is to behave like the pediatrician who should know better. It is necessary to move toward the recognition that a significant proportion of mothers become inadequate because the culture of alienation stands in the way of adequacy.

The validity of this observation is supported by van den Berg's (1972) social-psychological insight and interest in the changing nature of the human society. He has placed the whole responsibility for miscarriages and abortions in socialization on society as a whole. This position is consistent with his more inclusive view that society is the major culprit in the development of the neuroses: "neuroses are socioses."

Inadequacies in the socialization experiences of children may be understood, following van den Berg, as deficiences in the culture. Mothers are in a very real sense custodians of children for society and socialize them in accordance with prevailing conditions. What has since become evident from van den Berg's review of the *maternal deprivation* hypothesis is that mothering failures arise from an endemic attitude of ambivalence in the cultures of the West. A kind of uncertainty has eroded the fabric of culture, expressing itself in the individual as a *choice problem* in the face of contradictory values. One such contradiction, for example, is contained in the value of one's love for one's neighbor and the equally treasured value of competition with the same neighbor. Mothers become uncertain with regard to the directions in which they should move in socializing children. When this ambivalence in values is compounded with the public tutoring of mothers on how to indulge in the practiced love of their children, the complications that may be expected to arise are enormous. Practiced love and mothering can be expected to lead to an unusual degree of self-consciousness—a state which happens to be the direct opposite of the preferred and natural state of "primary maternal preoccupation."

By directing attention on schizoid phenomena, suggesting that in addition to the light the phenomena throw on socialization and body representation, the phenomena highlights the crucial social-psychological problem of the age—the divided and fragmented self of the culture of alienation. The most dramatic failures in socialization appear to have the greatest potential for activating splitting processes. Since mothers have been scapegoated for what would appear to be a cultural deficiency, it was necessary to deal with this aspect. From the point of view of alienation, the question arises whether it is realistic to account for man's experience of futility and helplessness on the basis mainly of spiritual categories, as Frankl does. While the spiritual dimension is unquestionably significant, the difference between the "noogenic neuroses" of Frankl and schizoid phenomena as described by various writers is seen as more semantic than real.

NOTES

1. It is remarkable how several workers writing from diverse interests and theoretical positions have converged on the notion of a divided self (van den Berg, Laing, Neumann, Reich). In different ways, they moved from a recognition and delineation of the "divided self" to formulations about cleavages in the collective experience or consciousness of large groups (van den Berg, Reich and Neumann).

2. The falsity of the character of the "body-for-others" is captured in Sartre's statement: An individual commited to a false bodily vitality "does not have a pure and simple consciousness of the massive modifications of his organs; the messages and appeals that his body sends him come with certain coefficients of ideality, and are always more or less symbolic of vital values. He even devotes a portion of his activity to procuring perceptions of himself that correspond to his vital ideal" (p. 120). It could be added here that the cultural development of the "body-for-others" has given rise to one of the most prosperous industries of the twentieth century—the cosmetics industry. The time spent on "procuring perceptions of himself that correspond to his vital ideal" is no longer a "portion" of his/her time but an increasingly significant one.

CHAPTER V

The Future of a Delusion

Much of the earlier analysis has been concentrated on establishing a number of important relationships, most important concerning the interplay between the development of civilization and the devaluation of the body. Investing the human body with an ambiguity unnatural to its existential givenness, has contributed to the progressive alienation of modern industrial man. Further, the essential aspects of thinking on man's alienation from his body were reduced to some developmental propositions intended to expose difficulties encountered by black and white children in the development of body representation. In both race supremacist cultures and socialization situations the existence of sociological schemata of the body were identified. Evident also was the fact that psychic splitting processes which are characteristic of industrial culture became replicated during socialization in the form of a split in body experience and representation. The most important conclusion derived from the analysis of all these relationships may be stated as follows. Alienation from the body is phenomenologically different in the black and white experiences of the body and its representation. In the white experience, alienation (devaluation and ambiguity) from the body led to two pseudo-solutions: the development of two sociological schemata. One captured the idealized, phantom, aristocratic and compensatory sociological schema identified with vital values. The other related to the devalued lower anal pole of the body associated with anti-values is projected outward. This sociological schema, in the history of colonalism and racism, developed into the sociological schemata of the black man and the Jew.

In terms of body experience, the Jew and the black man (victims of racism) dealt with the sociological schemata by unconsciously colluding with the racist, by actively devaluating their own body type while introjecting the vital values of the idealized white sociological schema; the black man more so than the Jew.

Popular opinion would lead one to believe that the end of the overtly colonial period in certain parts of Africa and elsewhere and the elimination of discriminatory practices against blacks in the Western world marked the end of racism against blacks. Informed opinion, on the other hand, leads to the understanding that what has been achieved in the United States, for example, according to Kovel (1970), is a shift from dominative racism through *aversive racism* to *metaracism*. He defines metaracism in the following terms:

> Metaracism, is then, the pursuit of consciously nonracist behavior in the interest of furthering the destructive work of culture. Under the terms of racism, the white self was either swollen, as in dominative racism, or pure, as in its aversive form, while the black person was less than a person, less than a self: either a concrete body-thing or, as time went on, a no-thing. In going beyond racism, one can raise both one's self and the other by a free act of mutual affirmation, grounded in a real human relationship in which both self and other are face to face, ends in themself. Or, as in

100

metaracism, one can reduce one's self: sell part to the culture, become a means to its end, and share this fate with people of other races (p. 215).[1]

Understanding the progression from dominative racism to metaracism suggests two important issues. First, in this development there is a refinement of racist behavior. Second, it is difficult to determine the extent to which the progression reflects a quantitative or qualitative reduction in racist behavior. But it is notable that the dominative racist thrived in the United States and in parts of Europe and Africa before independence when manifest social-political institutions existed to support racism and racist behavior. With the disappearance of those structures, the metaracist, sleeker in his ways, made his appearance.

In the United States, for instance, where institutional structures that supported racism have been eliminated, the dominative racist finds it difficult to survive and manifest his racist behavior except in overdramatized racial confrontations. Thus the metaracist may be expected to have a great potential for rapid regressions to dominative racist trends depending on the interracial interaction he may experience.

The dominative racist is not museum material—he exists and thrives shamelessly in Southern Africa. For in that part of the African continent, white minority governments and their constituencies have made racism the cardinal principle of sociopolitical organization. The psychopolitical elements of the South African scene are discussed elsewhere. Since the analysis here is primarily psychological and phenomenological, it will suffice to deal with South African society in the most general terms.

Since the landing of the first white settlers from Holland in 1652, successive white minority governments have compounded a predominantly colonial sociopolitical organization with a racist social system to continue white domination against the country's indigenous black majority. The manifest social structure of South African society consists of a system of monopolies of political, economic and military power. The policy of *apartheid* (separate development) is intended to achieve the separatist intentions of South African whites: the separation of blacks and whites in all spheres of life while ensuring the maintenance of white domination.

Since discrimination is written into all the laws of South Africa, it should not surprise anybody to learn that the most serious crime, atoned for by capital punishment for the black man, is not high treason but the rape of white women. While a political "offender" may earn the heroism of a life imprisonment or house arrest, he has the benefit of an internal sense of freedom, of self-transcendence and a future to look forward to, bleak as it may be. The rapist, or even more often the alleged rapist, of the white woman is sent to the gallows.[2] A white man who rapes a black woman arouses giggles and raises eyebrows in court and might even get away with murder.

The white man in South Africa still prides himself on his so-called "civilizing mission." He fails to recognize that what he brought from Europe is alienation which he calls Christianity and civilization. He often argues that the white man must maintain his position of domination in order to act as a bulwark against the spread of communism in Africa and to uphold the glorious achievements of Western civilization. In the white dominated countries of Southern Africa elaborate manifest sociopolitical institutions are being developed in support of white racism.[3] Within this context of white alienation and dehumanization, black and white children are brought up to equally profound kinds of alienation.

The alienation of the black man from his body within the South African context suggested itself in two studies involving children and adults (Manganyi, Kromberg and Jerkins, 1974; Manganyi, 1972). Since those studies, a great deal of energy and time has been devoted to the phenomenological study of body experience in race supremacist cultures (Manganyi, 1973). The phenomenological understanding of the black man's alienation from his body in the South African situation has been formulated in the following terms (Manganyi, 1973):

> It should be considered natural under these circumstances for an individual . . . to conceive of his body as something which is essentially undesirable (something unattractive); something which paradoxically must be kept at a distance outside of one's self so to speak. This paradoxical feat is, of course, never achieved in reality. It expresses itself in reality in a sort of diffuse body experience, a certain inarticulateness of the experience of the physical self. . . .
>
> A socio-cultural assault on the bodies of a whole people is perhaps one of the most vicious tragedies that can befall a people. This truth is simply illustrated. The physical body constitutes an individual's anchor in the world. It is the physical body which makes it possible for an individual to be given a name, to tell all and sundry who he is—to constitute lived space. The body is the nexus of all the fundamental relations (dialogue) which an individual . . . develops with others, with objects and with space and time. If the integrity of the body is violated, as it has been in the case of black people, the other existential relationships also become distorted. Integrity for the body is what a solid foundation means for a good house. Violate the integrity of this foundation (the body) and everything else collapses after the fact (pp. 51-52).

Although the alienation of the black man from his body, under racist conditions, may be expected to be more profound, the racist also suffers from a different kind of body alienation. The white South African racist is the victim of the cultural ambiguity and devaluation of his body. He passed this ambiguity and uneasiness onto the black man.

In both the situations of the black man and white man, the sociological schema of the body predominates over the individual schema; while the psychologically preferable situation would appear to be the reverse of this situation.

The South African situation teeming with dominative racists provides a dramatic contrast to situations where metaracism has become predominant. In both the racist and metaracist society, however, psychic splitting is significant in the process of scapegoating. In an important statement on "social systems as defense against persecutory and depressive anxiety," Elliott Jacques (1955) adds his opinion regarding the significance of personality splitting for the dynamics of scapegoating:

> Let us consider first certain aspects of the problem of the scapegoating of a minority group. As seen from the viewpoint of the community at large, the community is split into a good majority and a bad minority—a split consistent with the splitting of internal objects into good and bad, and the creation of a good and bad internal world. The persecuting group's belief in its own good is preserved by heaping contempt upon and attacking the scapegoated group. The internal splitting mechanisms and preservation of the internal good objects of individuals, and the attack upon, and contempt for, internal, bad prosecutory objects, are reinforced by introjective identification of individuals with other members taking part in the group-sanctioned attack upon the scapegoat (p. 485).

This statement represents, for Jacques, the core problem of social change. He proceeds to argue that what accounts for the difficulties encountered in attempts to introduce social change arise because of failures to recognize what he describes as the "fantasy social structure" which accompanies the manifest structure of social systems. In any form

104

of institutional organization, there is in addition to what the society recognizes as the rationale for the institution(s), an irrational and unconscious investment by the group in the system thus created.[4] It is imperative in the analysis of groups and social systems to identify the two crucial elements of manifest structure and fantasy structure. The one is readily available to observation while the latter is unconscious and constitutes a defense mechanism against tension-producing levels of anxiety.

Within the context of this framework, we begin to understand how the dominative racist becomes a metaracist. It requires no unusual insight to realize that a metaracist may very well continue to be afflicted with unconscious racist fantasies that have survived the changes in manifest social organization. He remains a social risk because, in racially extreme situations, he can always be expected to regress into the dominative mold. This kind of social regression was dramatized in France where an incident involving a black deviant almost started a wave of racial violence. The significance of all this is that institutional changes involving political, social and economic systems represent an essential beginning in the process of social change. To eradicate racism in the institutional life of a society is not sufficient to demystify the unconscious ramifications involved in the fantasy social structure underlying such systems. But in clinical experience, patients in psychotherapy desperately resist the possible loss of their neuroses. On the collective level, the difficulties of working through the fantasy social structure supporting racism raises many practical problems which society prefers to ignore.

In any one situation, it becomes almost impossible, because of problems relating to political and economic group interests, to approach the problem of racism at both the levels of manifest social institutional structure and fantasy structure. The manifest institutional structure of racism in South Africa, for example, is the most observable and would appear on rational grounds to be amenable to rational restructuring. It should be clear by now that racist minority systems will ultimately prove counter-productive. But rationality, a vision of the future and a profound sense of history are all unavailable to the white racist minorities in Southern Africa. There is enough evidence in the history of colonial and other forms of racism to suggest that the institutional structures supporting racism are rarely changed by reform but by revoluntionary means.

At the institutional level, radical transformations may occur within a relatively short time. Radical change in the political, social, and economic institutions of a society may be restructured to meet unexpected demands for a share of power and opportunity which may result from civil rights legislation for example. The reality and feasibility of this possibility was demonstrated by the history of colonial racism. But the eradication of the fantasy social structure would appear by the nature of its complexity to require evolutionary strategies. Focus on the fantasy social structure will become more imperative with the final elimination of dominative racism in those parts of the world where it still exists. As long as the unconscious elements remain unaddressed, the world will have to contend with metaracists who will always be victims of a possible dangerous social regression. Another danger is the tendency of powerful individuals and groups to resist institutional change on the false pretext that such change is difficult to come by. This view confuses passion with analysis; for it is possible to free the victim of racism while allowing the racist to thrive on his alienation. The two situations as transitional stages in the process of change are not incompatible.

From a social-psychological perspective, the core element in the alienation of man in industrial society is the split in his consciousness of his nature. In psychodynamic terms, the state of being alienated can be seen to have developed by elevating the mechanism of repression into a virtue in the organization of society. This state of virtue was achieved at great costs to individuals and groups. The general result was an amputated status of a whole sphere of man's nature and existence that was denied and devalued. Man imposed unnatural and disjunctive limitations on aspects of his nature. These aspects progressively became lost to man's conscious awareness. The vitality of the body was the primary victim of this massive ethical devaluation and subsequent repression. The resulting alienation of man from his body assumed a specific form; a character which replicated the old ethic's two-valued orientation towards reality.

The alienation of modern industrial man from his body receives a concrete expression within the context of the socialization of children. The family with its placement function of socializing children for society actually does a good job of diffusing the cultural values and attitudes relating to the body. For the mother and the family socializing a child, society has developed and systematized its alienation from the body in clearly discernable ways. The most advanced cultures became the most rigorous in their expectations for acceptable patterns of dealing with the body's vital functions. Rational and irrational processes combined to create some of the most demanding taboos and superstitions about sexuality, menstruation, and excrement. Anti-values such as those relating to dirt, smell and evil were completely elaborated and dramatically attached to the lower pole of the body.[5] Not all socialization experiences regarding anal cleanliness, for example, are equally traumatic to children, as Newmann (1973) has emphasized:

> The sense of being unclean is intensified, however, when the cultural canon and its ideal of cleanliness provoke a feeling

of guilt, of sinfulness and uncleanness, so that the anal pole becomes identified with obligatory magical rituals for the elimination of evil.

Commenting on the problem of anal rejection:

> Thus the experience of original sin, of one's own inferiority, characteristics of patriarchal Judeo-Christian culture, is related to the negatively evaluated animal element in man's own nature to the fact that man is unclean, born *intre urinas et faeces*. To have a body means to possess a lower negative body pole belonging to the earth, whereas such heavenly spiritual beings as the angels have only an upper body and a head-pole (p. (p. 128).

The existence of anti-values of the body was counterpoised with a compensatory *body aesthetic* which, in the course of cultural history, has moved from purely idealistic formulation in the arts to the television image of the cosmetics industry. A body that is beautiful and graceful but smells is cognitively dissonant.

The ambiguity characteristic of the sociological schema of the body is brought to bear on the child's developing body representation. The alienation from the body and the subsequent ambiguity led to the development of the negative sociological body schemata of the black man and the Jew in racist societies. White societies have only been convinced, in a very superficial sense, about the "aristocracy" or wholesomeness of the human body. Body anxiety, according to some experts is a common problem for individuals in the most advanced industrial cultures (Fisher, 1973). The primary demand for an improvement in this situation would appear to be one that would ensure the explorations of ways to reduce and eliminate the artificial ambiguity in the culture as well. Most adults would agree, on the basis of their own experience with their bodies, that the elimination of ambiguity and anxiety around body experience would, indeed, be a very demanding task.

But it seems better to think in this direction than to wait for a universal pop music festival to resurrect man's interest and awareness of the complex reality of his body, as suggested in Cleaver's (1968) observation:

> The stiff, mechanical Omnipotent Administrators and Ultrafeminines presented a startling spectacle as they entered in droves onto the dance floors to learn how to Twist. They came from every level of society, from top to bottom, writhing pitifully though gamely about the floor, feeling exhiliarating and soothing new sensations, released from some unknown prison in which their Bodies had been encased, a sense of freedom they had never known before, a feeling of communion with some mystical root-source of life and vigor, from which sprang a new awareness and enjoyment of the flesh, a new appreciation of the possibilities of their Bodies (p. 197).

Here is a profound vision which got lost. It is important to follow this kind of insight with an exploration of how education as secondary socialization could help society deal with the problems of the *ambiguous body*. Perhaps the body requires as much attention as the ego in the education of children. The person-ego or self must be developed wholly. Such an effort would not only help eliminate the sociological schemata of the body which interfere with the development of positive and healthy body representation, but it would counterbalance the effects of parental influences in the family situation.

Ego splitting during development cannot be completely eliminated, but its body representation elements could be reduced. The institutional scapegoat—the black or Jewish sociological schemata of the body—could also be actively wiped out. It seems that it is not sufficient for parents to tell children that the black man or the Jew is a man in his own right while nourishing the symbolic matrix associated with these groups. The benefits for society of reducing the ambiguity of the body and the associated anxiety are of significance apart from considerations relating to the problem of the scapegoat psychology. To Frankl's belief that what alienated man needs to do to improve his condition is to confront meaning, should be added the need for confronting the body. Authenticity will only be available to those who, in the midst of a cultural chaos in many areas of modern life, still find it possible to be fully conscious of the various aspects of the existential structure. Full liberation of the white body from ambiguity—a new trend in socialization and education which would focus on the irradication of the body's devaluation—means that the deceptive sociological schema of the white body, pitted against the anti-values of the lower anal pole of the body, should be formulated more realistically. What this would mean in practice is that the current polarization in body representation in growing children would be reduced. Its place should be taken by a unified representation of the body. There is an additional condition.

The liberation of the white body, the thawing of the anxiety and irrationality surrounding the body, is also contingent on the elimination of values of comparison which created the sociological schemata of the bodies of the victims of racism. Here, the responsibility for the liberation of the black body from devaluation and its own peculiar form of ambiguity, rests on the shoulders of blacks the world over. We have said that the black child may be expected to experience additional problems in the development of its body representation. *Black consciousness* must continue to address itself to the liberation of the black body. The negative sociological schema of the black body must be destroyed once and for all. A short "black is beautiful" campaign is not sufficient in itself to bring about this liberation of the body. A campaign of this kind must be sufficiently in-

110

tegrated into broader politicosocial strategies and planning. Even of more importance is the systematic exploration of educational opportunities for positive body consciousness raising. Most educational systems have formats for physical education that could provide necessary body related education. No educational system known to the author has teachers who are sufficiently sophisticated to be of much help to children with problems in the development of their body representation and awareness. Those countries in the Western world such as the United States that have eliminated the manifest institutional structures of racism may realize an important responsibility by leading the way in the exploration of the possibilities of the educational situation with regard to the problem of the body.

The liberation of the body from its ambiguity in both the racist and the victim of racism must be achieved simultaneously. The sociological schemata must be removed from public consciousness (both conscious and unconscious) on both sides in order for change to be significant.

Where the institutional manifest structures of racism have been destroyed, there is a need for attempting to deal with the unconscious fantasy structure. One way to begin is to approach the problem of scapegoating from the point of view of the body and its cultural and experienced ambiguity. The attack on the recalcitrant unconscious elements in racist behavior should not be left entirely to chance. In societies where racism is still the preferred principle of social organization, there are hardly any choices left but for revolutionary change. Changes must be effected quickly for freedom and dignity to be gained. In these cases, the manifest structures must be changed while the problem of the fantasy social structure must be left for the future.

Racism is an aberration of alienated industrial man. It has been a delusion of racial superiority which has cost the world a great deal in human potential and grandeur of stature. Is there a beyond racism? Certainly not while the alienation of man continues to thrive. The best that can be hoped for in the present condition is *containment*. Hopefully, killing on a large scale, supporting a delusional racial superiority, will never again become a human possibility.[6]

NOTES

1. In all varities of racism as well as the general condition of alienation, the individual is coerced to sell part of his self to the culture. It is in this way that the alienated worker became a means to the ends of culture and civilization. This means, *inter alia,* that a depth psychological theory of alienation, supported by sound sociology, must also say that man's alienation from his body arose when man began to believe that he could sacrifice his body to culture;—when the body became a means to the ends of culture, it became lost to the individual.

2. See Kovel's *White Racism* (1970) for a discussion of the experience of Afro-Americans in this regard.

3. The most recent elaboration is the institutionalization of tribalism expressed in the South African version of so-called "African homelands." Various African tribes are being hurdled into scattered bits of land as part of a grand design to create "independent" tribal states, separated from what is described as "white South Africa" consisting mainly of the large industrial and agricultural centers and the sea shore.

4. The irrational and "unconscious fantasy structure" and aspects relating to the body-world are not the only factors to account for racism. Overtly economic & political factors must also be considered.

5. See Kovel (1970) and Neumann's *The Child* (1973) for discussions of this symbolic matrix.

6. "State" murders are found in association with policies supporting racism. In such instances, deficiency diseases take their toll of the victims of racism and are treated with a respect accorded policies directed at family planning.

CHAPTER VI

Epilogue

> "Resign yourself to your color the way I got used to my stump; we're both victims."

This statement, from *Home of the Brave* (cited by Fanon, 1967, p. 140), can be taken for an important metaphor which captures most of what has been said here about alienation, the body and racism.

The amputee resists integration of the loss of a body part. He indulges himself by developing a ghost limb (amputation phantom). The amputation of a body part is in reality, more than a simple physical act. It represents a disruption of a psychic *gestalt;* a whole and unitary representation of the body. The amputee fares better than you and I, because in the best of clinical situations, he comes to terms with his amputation. Modern industrial man in conditions different from those of the amputee effected a psychological amputation by denying the reality of the vitality of the body. Through a process of substitution and compensation, he developed a phantom body representation (sociological schema) which gave him a deceptive impression of wholeness and unity. The phantom and hallucinatory character of the sociological schema is still

113

reflected by the ambiguity and anxiety which man experiences with regard to his body.

By referring to the psychosocial context of the origins of alienation we have attempted to place the development of the devaluation of the body, the emergence of ambiguity and anxiety around the body, in the general context of a symbol system which has been essentially dualistic and two-valued. We have also emphasized the fact that the colonizer was already alienated from his body by the time he made contact with blacks. The colonizer institutionalized racism as part of an elaboration of this alienation.

In different historical and cultural contexts, the scapegoating of the black man and the Jew were, in complex ways, coping mechanisms: an attempt by the racist to deal with tensions that had developed as a result of psychic splitting. Since the Aryan body had already been polarized on the basis of vital values (upper body pole) and anti-values (anal lower pole), this split into"good" and "bad" in the collective psyche required resolution. Good objects are generally internalized while bad objects are driven out of conscious awareness. As we know, the tensions promoted by this split lead to the return of the repressed in one form or another. It is this split and its tensions which led to the creation of the negative sociological body schemata of the black man and the Jew. The Jew and the black man became their "brother's keeper" by becoming the repositories of the anti-values of the lower pole of the Aryan body.

The split between "good" and "bad" objects also develops with respect to body representation during development. The formulations on the development of body representation are provided because of a number of reasons. First, it is now theoretically possible to integrate what is known from other disciplines about the body image into our theories not only of development, in general, but, more specifically, the evolution of ego consciousness: ego-object relations and representation. Reductionism in formulations on the person constellation is no longer justifiable in view of the current sophistication of the body image literature. Secondly, the characterization of the development of body representation which was given suggests that socialization in race supremacist cultures is riddled with a symbolic matrix intertwined with polarizations in body attitudes and unrealistic sociological schemata of the body. The development of a healthy, unambiguous and less anxiety-provoking body representation is currently made difficult and complex for both the white child who grows up into a racist and the black child who, as the victim of racism) colludes and shares the alienation of his white counterpart.

Finally, the dynamics surrounding the development of individual and sociological schemata of the body and the dynamic formulations of others (Kubie, 1965; Fanon, 1967; Pinderhughes, 1969; Kovel, 1970; Fisher, 1973) reveal that there exists a complex fantasy structure which has supported both culture and institutionalized racism. We singled out one element in this fantasy structure because of our theoretical interest and emphasis on body representation. The other aspects of dehumanization in racist black-white interaction have received a great deal of attention in the literature to require any further documentation. It is necessary, though, to emphasize that all the elements of the fantasy structure such as the sexual fantasies which have determined the pattern of the social structuring of racist societies, should be taken into full account in any effort directed at social change. The emphasis on the body is partly dictated by the conviction that the devaluation of the body is one of the core elements of the alienated condition and the prevailing fantasy social structure which creates the scapegoat.

A possible approach to the gradual elimination of the fantasy social structure supporting racism within the socialization matrix was suggested. When passion will have settled, man will be able to say what in our time is being said in muted tones: in any racist social structure there is so much infection that it becomes difficult to sift the victims from the carriers. Because of this, visions of the future which are overly optimistic about racism may be more "romantic" than real. One should understand that the solution of the problem of racism requires for its effectiveness the elimination of the main virus—alienation.

REFERENCES

Allport, G.W. *Becoming: Basic considerations for a psychology of personality.* New Haven: Yale University Press, 1955.

Benton, A.L. *Right-left discrimination and finger localization: Development and pathology.* Hoeber & Harper, 1959.

Berg, van den, J. H. "Verantwoording." In J. H. van den Berg & J. Linschoten (Red.): *Persoon en Wereld: Bijdragen tot de phaenomenologisghe psychologie.* Ubrecht: E. J. Bijleveld, 1953.

————: "Living in plurality." *Humanitas: Journal of the Institute of Man,* VII, 3, 1971; 395-409.

————: "What is Psychotherapy?" *Humanitas: Journal of the Institute of Man,* VII, 3, 1971b, 321-370.

————: *Dubious Maternal Affection.* Pittsburgh: Duquesne University Press, 1972.

Blatt, S. & Ritzler, B. A. "Thought disorder and body boundary disturbances in psychoses." *Journal of Consulting and Clinical Psychology,* 1974, 42, 3, 370-388.

Brown, N.O. *Life against death: The psychoanlytic meaning of history.* New York: Vintage Books, 1959.

————: *Love's Body.* New York: Vintage Books, 1966.

Camus, A.: *The Myth of Sisyphus and other essays.* New York: Vintage Books, 1955.

————: *The Rebel.* New York: Vintage Books, 1956.

Cleaver, E. *Soul on Ice.* New York: Delta, 1968.

Coles, R. "When I draw the Lord he'll be a real big man." In M. Wertheimer (ed.), *Confrontation: Psychology and the problems of today.* Scott, Foresman & Co., Glenview, Illinois; 1970, 102-113.

Critchley, M. *The parietal lobes.* London: Edward Arnold, 1953.

Cytrynbaum, S. "Black-white interpersonal dynamics: A selective review," 1972 (unpublished).

Deutsch, M., Katz, I. & Jensen, A.R. (eds.). *Social class, race, and psychological development:* New York: Holt, Rinehart & Winston, 1968.

Erickson, E. H. : *Identity: Youth and Crisis.* New York: Norton & Company, 1968.

Fairbairn, W.R.D. *An object-relations theory of the personality.* New York: Basic Books, 1954.

Fanon, F. *Black skin white masks.* New York: Grove Press, 1967.

Fisher, S. Body image boundaries and hallucinations. In L.J. West (ed.): *Hallucinations.* New York: Grune & Stratton, 1962, 249-260.

————: A further appraisal of the body boundary concept. *Journal of Consulting Psychology,* 1963, 27, 62-74.

————: *Body experience in fantasy and behavior.* New York: Appleton-Century-Crofts, 1970.

————: *Body consciousness: You are what you feel.* Englewood Cliffs, New Jersey: Prentice-Hall, 1973.

Fisher, S. & Cleveland, S. E. *Body image and personality* (2nd ed.). Princeton, New Jersey: D. Van Nostrand, 1968.

Frankl, V. *The doctor and the soul.* New York: Alfred Knopf, 1965.

————: *Psychotherapy and existentialism: Selected papers on Logotherapy.* New York: Simon & Schuster, 1967.

Fromm, E. *Escape from freedom.* New York: Holt, Rinehart and Winston, 1941.

Gerstmann, J. "Syndrome of finger agnosia, disorientation for right and left, agraphia and acalculia." *Archives of Neurology and Psychiatry,* 1940, 44, 398-408.

————: "Problem of imperception of disease and of impaired body territories with organic lesions." *Archives of Neurology and Psychiatry,* 1942, 48, 890-913.

————: "Some notes on the Gerstmann syndrome." *Neurology,* 1957, 7, 866-869.

————: "Psychological and pheomenological aspects of disorders of the body image." *Journal of Nervous and Mental Disease,* 1958, 126, 499-512.

Gladstone, I. "On the aetiology of depersonalization." *Journal of Nervous and Mental Disease,* 1947, 105, 25.

Goodman, M. *Rage awareness in young children.* New York: Collier Books, 1964.

Gorman, W.H. *Body image and the image of the brain.* St. Louis, Missouri: Warren H. Green, 1969.

Guntrip, H. *Psychoanalytic theory, therapy and the self.* New York: Basic Books, 1971.

Hamilton, J. "Some dynamics of anti-Negro prejudice." *Psychoanalytic Review,* LII, 1966-1967, 5-15.

Jalavisto, E. "Adaptation in the phantom limb phenomenon as influenced by the age of the amputee." *Journal of Gerontology,* 1950, 5, 339.

Kolb, L.C. "Disturbances of the body image." In S. Arieti (ed.): *American Handbook of Psychiatry.* New York: Basic Books, 1959, 749-769.

———: "Phantom sensations, hallucinations and the body image." In L.J. West (ed.) *Hallucinations.* New York: Grune & Stratton, 1962, 239-248.

Kouwer, B.J. "Gelaat en Karakter." In J.H. van den Berg & J. Linschoten (Red.): *Persoon en wereld: Bijdragen tot de phaenomenologische psychologie.* Utrecht: Erven J. Bijleveld, 1953, 59-73.

Kovel, J. *White racism: A psychohistory.* New York: Vintage Books, 1970.

Kubie, L. "The ontogeny of racial prejudice." *Journal of Nervous and Mental Disease,* CXLI, 1965, 265-273.

Laing, R.D. *The divided self.* Penguin Books, 1959.

———: *The politics of experience.* New York: Ballantine Books, 1967.

Jacques, E. "Social Systems as defense against persecutory and depressive anxiety." In: M. Klein, et al. (eds.): *New Directions in Psychoanalysis.* New York: Basic Books, 1955, 478-498.

Manganyi, N.C. "Body image boundary differentiation and self-steering behavior in African Paraplegics." *Journal of Personality Assessment,* 36, 1, 1972, 45-50.

———: *Being-black-in-the-world.* Johannesburg: Sprocas-Ravan, 1973.

Manganyi, N.C., Kromberg, J.A. & Jenkins, T: "Studies on Albinism in the South African Negro 1. — Intellectual Maturity and Body Image Differentiation." *Journal of Biosocial Science,* 6, 1974, 107-112.

Marcuse, H. *Eros and civilization.* Boston: Beacon Press, 1955.

McDonald, M. *Not by the color of their skin.* New York: International Universities Press, 1970.

Merleau-Ponty, M.: Phenomenology of Perception. London: Routledge & Kegan Paul, 1962.

———: *The primacy of perception.* J.M. Edie (ed.): Northwestern University Press, 1964.

Neumann, E. *The origins and history of consciousness.* Princeton, New Jersey: Princeton University Press, 1954.

———: *Psychology and a new ethic.* New York: Harper Torchbooks, 1973 (first English translation, 1969).

———: *The child: Structure and dynamics of the nascent personality.* G.P. Putnam's Sons, 1973.

Pinderhughes, C. "Understanding Black Power: Processes and proposals." *American Journal of Psychiatry,* CXXV, 1969, 1552-7.

Reich, W. *The mass psychology of fascism.* New York: Farrar, Straus & Giroux, 1970 (new translation by V.R. Carfangno).

Sartre, J.P. *Anti-Semite and Jew.* New York: Schocken Books, 1948.

Schilder, P. *The image and appearance of the human body.* New York: International Universities Press, 1950 (first published, 1935).

———: *Contributions to developmental neuropsychiatry.* New York: International Universities Press, 1964.

Shontz, F.C. *Perceptual and cognitive aspects of body experience.* New York: Academic Press, 1969.

Simmel, M.L. "Phantom experiences following amputation in childhood." *Journal of Neurology, Neurosurgery and Psychiatry,* 1962, 25, 69.

Slater, P.E.: "On social regression." *American Sociological Review,* Vol. 28, 3, 1963, 339-64.

Stern, M. & Robbins, E.S. "Clinical diagnosis and treatment of psychiatric disorders subsequent to use of psychedelic drugs." In R.E. Hicks & P.J. Fink (eds.): *Psychedelic drugs.* New York: Grune & Stratton, 1969, 55-65.

Szasz, T.S. *Pain and pleasure.* New York: Basic Books, 1957.

Winnicott, D.W. *Mother and child.* New York: Basic Books, 1957.

———: *Collected papers.* New York: Basic Books, 1958.

Witkin, H.A., Dyk, R.B., Faterson, H.F., Goodenough, D.R. & Karp, S.A. *Psychological differentiation: Studies of development.* New York: John Wiley & Sons, 1962.

INDEX

Pare, A., 10, 57
Pentagon, 5
Pinderhughes, C., 9, 115
Psychoanalysis, 8, 20
Psychohistory, 8

Reich, W., 40, 41, 42, 53, 80, 97
Rhodesia, 16
Ritzler, B., 60, 61
Robbins, E., 12

St. Peter's Cathedral, 5
Sartre, J., 45, 46, 47, 48, 49, 53, 97
Schilder, P., 10, 11, 14, 16, 57, 58, 62, 67
Separate Development, 54, 102
Sheehan, E., 6
Shontz, F., 16, 58

Simmel, M., 11
Sisyphus, 5
Slater, P., 16
South Africa, 16, 49, 52, 53, 54, 77, 102, 106
Southern Africa, 6, 16, 53, 101, 102, 106
Stern, M., 12
Sullivan, H., 59
Szasz, T., 57

United States of America, 100, 101, 111

Vervooerd, B., 7, 49
Vorster, J., 15

Winnicott, D., 59, 92, 93, 94
Witkin, H., 58, 78